What Works in Preventing Rural Violence

Strategies, Risk Factors, and Assessment Tools

Prepared by:

Barbara Monsey, M.P.H.
Greg Owen, Ph.D.
Carol Zierman, B.S.
Laura Lambert, M.A.
Vincent Hyman

Wilder Research Center

Amherst H. Wilder Foundation
St. Paul, Minnesota

We thank the Blandin Foundation, Grand Rapids, Minnesota,
for underwriting the development of this book

This research summary was developed by Wilder Research Center, a program of the Amherst H. Wilder Foundation in St. Paul, Minnesota. The report was developed in collaboration with the Blandin Foundation, located in the rural community of Grand Rapids, Minnesota.

The Amherst H. Wilder Foundation is one of the largest and oldest endowed human service agencies in America. For more than eighty years, the Wilder Foundation has provided human services responsive to the welfare needs of the community, all without regard to or discrimination on account of nationality, sex, color, or religious scruples.

The mission of the Blandin Foundation is to strengthen rural Minnesota communities. It was established in 1941 by the pioneering newspaper man, Charles K. Blandin. The Blandin Foundation provides grants, conferencing programs for the discussion of issues, and leadership and training programs for community leaders. To contact the Blandin Foundation, call (218) 326-0523.

We hope you find this report helpful! If you want to purchase additional copies, please mail or fax the order form in the back of this book or call:

Toll Free 1 (800) 274-6024

If you have questions about the research, contact:

Wilder Research Center
1295 Bandana Boulevard North, Suite 210
St. Paul, MN 55108

Phone (612) 647-4600

Researched and written by Barbara R. Monsey, M.P.H., Greg Owen, Ph.D., Carol Zierman, B.S., Laura Lambert, M.A., and Vincent Hyman.
Designed by Rebecca Andrews
Cover illustration by Greg Preslicka

Manufactured in the United States of America

Library of Congress Cataloging-in-Publication Data

What works in preventing rural violence : strategies, risk
    factors, and assessment tools / prepared by Barbara
    Monsey... [et al.] (Wilder Research Center).
        p.   cm.
    Includes bibliographic references and index.
    ISBN 0-940069-04-0 (pbk.)
    1. Rural crimes--United States--Prevention.
2. Violence--United States--Prevention. 3. Crime
prevention--United States. I. Wilder Research Center.
II. Amherst H. Wilder Foundation.
HV6791.W53 1995
364.4'0973'091734--dc20   94-49041

PRINTED ON RECYCLED PAPER
10% POSTCONSUMER WASTE

ACKNOWLEDGMENTS

The authors wish to thank Don Streufert and the Blandin Foundation whose vision and confidence in us made this project a reality. We also wish to thank Kathryn Jensen and Don Bargen, whose thoughtful advice helped us to maintain our focus on rural communities. We are grateful for the support of our many colleagues at Wilder Research Center, especially Marilyn Conrad, Louann Graham, and Darlene Trumble, who helped prepare this manuscript; Kent Treichel, who provided crime statistics; and Paul Mattessich, who encouraged publishing this work and provided helpful advice. We thank Vince Hyman of the Wilder Publishing Center whose editing skills helped us produce a much stronger report. ∎

CONTENTS

FOREWORD

What does it take to do something about violence in rural communities? In our case, it was the abduction, rape, and murder of our nineteen-year-old daughter.

These crimes occurred in our rural Minnesota community, and the victims and offenders were residents of the same community. These tragic and criminal acts ignited our rural community to ask, "How can this horror occur and how can these acts be prevented in the future?"

In pursuit of its mission to strengthen rural communities, the Blandin Foundation of Grand Rapids, Minnesota, initiated Pathways to Peace and Safety to determine how the Foundation's resources could be used to address violence in rural communities. We began by asking local service providers to help us understand what was being done for victims, offenders, and the prevention of violence. Long conversations ensued. It soon became evident that many resources were already being expended, and service providers from many disciplines were committed to reducing violence. However, these providers were not aware of what others had found to be effective. None of us knew how much research had been done, what the key findings were, and where these were being applied. Most important, there was no single source that told us what kinds of efforts had been successful at reducing violence in rural communities.

We searched beyond our own community to agencies with a statewide focus. We found capable and committed staff, but they had only a limited knowledge of violence in rural communities. They encouraged us to document how violence was being effectively addressed in rural communities.

Through the help of Jane Gilgun at the University of Minnesota, we were introduced to Greg Owen at the Wilder Research Center. He and his colleagues had extensive experience in evaluating programs aimed at reducing violence in urban settings. Further, they had the expertise and capability to review the literature for effective strategies to respond to rural violence. They examined the literature on violence in rural communities with professional precision, with a passion sparked by our own grief, and with compassion for all who are victimized by violence.

The result is a document that informs and heals. It exposes gaps and generates hope. It illuminates the broad causes of violence and the impacts of specific interventions. It expands the search for what effectively reduces violence in all communities. It helps us to understand what works, for whom, and in what locale.

It is a significant step along the pathways to greater peace and safety.

Don and Mary Streufert
Pathways to Peace and Safety
Blandin Foundation

PREFACE

The core of this report was originally prepared for Pathways to Peace and Safety. That organization, whose mission is to reduce violence in rural areas, is sponsored by the Blandin Foundation of Grand Rapids, Minnesota. We believe the report, which was a first step for Pathways, can be used by rural areas across North America to respond to and reduce violence.

An article of faith is that at the grassroots level, we can do much to improve our situation. Information is the starting point; we must understand the nature of violence in our communities. In this report we collect and distill some of what is known about violence. The focus is on small communities, their residents, and their encounters with violence. We hope that this information will help rural communities begin to:

- Name and monitor peacemaking and violence in their communities.

- Understand how they administer restorative justice.

- Raise nonviolent children.

- Achieve and celebrate reconciliation, equity, and inclusion among diverse people.

We begin with the assumption that our real-life experiences with violence are both hurtful and costly. We ask: What can be done to stem the tide of violence in small communities? What has been of demonstrated value in reducing violence or mitigating its effects? How do we best serve those touched by violence? How can we pay attention to what is going on in our communities in a way that can lead to a reduction in the frequency, pain, and monetary costs of violence? ■

Why Look at Violence in Rural Communities?

V iolence is everywhere in America, or so it seems. From daily newspapers to academic journals, from cartoons to cinema, from popular music to personal experience, violence is a pervasive force in our lives. And while urban violence grabs the headlines and often makes our cities seem like armed camps, rural America also suffers from the culture of violence and its lasting effects.

Our culture celebrates rural life as free from the stress and danger of urban life. It is true that on average, smaller cities, suburban areas, and rural counties do have lower rates of violent crime than large metropolitan areas. But rural America is far from free of violence, and more important, violent crime is on the increase in all communities. From 1965 to 1992, the rape, robbery, and assault rates *tripled* in rural communities, according to U.S. Department of Justice statistics.

Changes in Rates of Violent Crime (Rape, Robbery, Assault) for Rural Communities* 1965 – 1992[1]

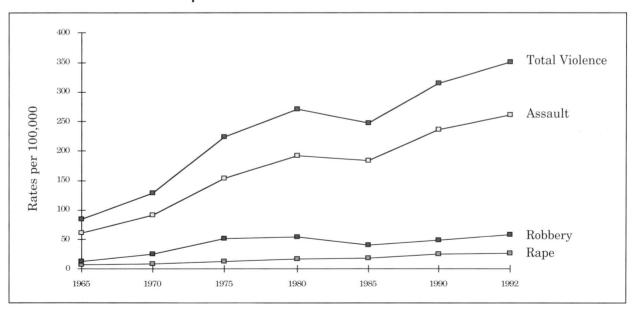

* Population of 24,999 or less.

[1] U.S. Department of Justice, Bureau of Justice Statistics. *Sourcebook of Criminal Justice Statistics,* 1965, 1970, 1975, 1980, 1985, 1990, 1992, Washington, D.C.

In a recent Department of Justice publication, Steven Dillingham, the Director of the Bureau of Justice Statistics writes,

The prevalence and nature of crime in rural America are important issues that, until recently, have received little attention. As nearly a quarter of the U.S. population resides in rural areas, crime in our nation's countryside threatens many individuals.[2]

It was not until 1992 that the Department of Justice attempted to summarize what was known about rural crime, particularly violent crime, in comparison to what was known about criminal activity in city and suburban areas. Using the National Crime Victimization Survey (NCVS), the Bureau's recent report examined the violent crimes of rape, robbery, aggravated assault, and simple assault based on individual household experiences with crime in the six months preceding the survey. The report shows the following:

- Rural areas account for approximately 16 percent of all violent crime in the United States.

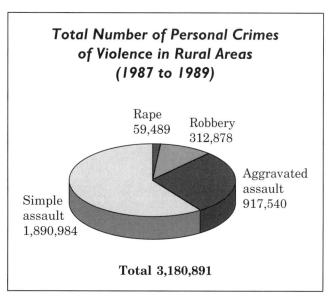

Total Number of Personal Crimes of Violence in Rural Areas (1987 to 1989)

Rape 59,489
Robbery 312,878
Aggravated assault 917,540
Simple assault 1,890,984

Total 3,180,891

- In rural areas, the rate of victimization by violent crimes was greater for whites than for persons of color.

- Rural victims of violence report that their assailant is more often a relative or acquaintance whereas city and suburban victims were more likely to report that a stranger had been the assailant.

- Rape is much more likely to be perpetrated by a person who is using alcohol at the time of the crime in rural communities than in either suburban or city communities (82.6 percent alcohol involvement in rural areas versus 62.4 percent in suburban areas and 51.0 percent in cities).

- In many categories of violent crime, including rape, robbery, aggravated assault, and simple assault, rural victims were more likely to report that the perpetrator was using alcohol than in either city or suburban areas.

- The National Crime Victimization Survey found that although women residing in central cities were more vulnerable to all types of violent crime, women living in rural areas have the same risk as women in

[2] U.S. Department of Justice (June 1992) "Crime Victimization in City, Suburban, and Rural Areas."

urban areas of experiencing an act of violence by an intimate partner. Women living in central cities, suburban areas, and rural locations experienced similar rates of violence committed by intimates.[3]

These facts suggest that violence in rural communities deserves careful study and response.

What Price Do We Pay for Violence?

There are many ways to think about the costs associated with violence. Older community residents often reflect on a time when they could walk alone at night or feel safe anywhere in their own town. The loss of this feeling of safety in a community is one cost of violence.

Consider the value of lives lost or damaged through violent actions. For example, how do we calculate the expenses associated with the sexual abuse of a child? Do we consider the cost of medical examination and treatment, social service interventions, and counseling for the victim? Do we also include the costs of police and court interventions for the perpetrator? Do we add the expense of subsequent incarceration and loss of family income?

Consider the murder of a young college graduate and the potential earnings lost, the police and court costs associated with the criminal investigation, the dollar value of prison time, and the social and psychological consequences for those left behind. There is no easy calculation that represents the value of these broken lives to members of a community or family.

While attempts to put a price on the aftermath of violence may seem callous and trivial to those whose lives have been touched in a much more profound and enduring way, such efforts are nonetheless useful. An advisory panel to a national study of violence was asked to develop costs associated with rape, robbery, and assault. The panel examined expenses for emergency room services, medical care, rehabilitation, absence from work, and property loss. The panel estimated costs of $16,500 for assault, $19,200 for robbery, and $54,100 for rape (see chart above).

Similar to the costs associated with a particular crime, the costs associated with the prosecution of criminals is astonishing. Consider, for

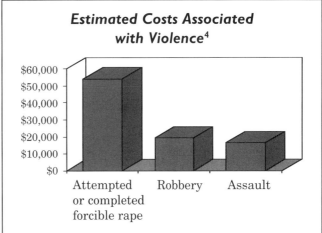

Estimated Costs Associated with Violence[4]

---

[3] Bachman (1994) *Violence Against Women, A National Crime Victimization Survey Report*

[4] In this example, 15 percent of costs are monetary losses and 85 percent are imputed costs for nonmonetary losses like pain, suffering, psychological damage, and reduced quality of life.

example, the judicial branch of the State of Minnesota. In 1990, it spent an estimated 175.1 million dollars—a cost of about forty-two dollars for each person living in the state.[5] This figure includes *only* the cost of running the courts and not the incarceration of offenders. (Incarceration at a Minnesota State correctional facility is a minimum of $40,000 per inmate per year.)

Finally, it is possible to think of the cost of violence in terms of court judgments against offenders. Given the great variation in violent crimes, it is not surprising that damage awards can vary from a few thousand dollars to several million dollars, depending upon medical bills, suffering inflicted, and permanency of damage.

Clearly, violence is expensive. It is expensive to police our communities, install security equipment in our homes and offices, staff our courts, build and maintain jails and prisons, help victims, and provide rehabilitation services for offenders.

Reducing violence can result in financial savings for communities. According to a Prentky and Burgess 1990 study, there is an estimated savings to society of $67,989 for treating a child molester rather than not.[6] Similarly, the National Research Council reported on a study showing that a sports and recreation program located in a housing project was far less expensive than the previous cost of juvenile criminal behavior. Likewise, community-based juvenile corrections programs were found to be quite effective in reducing recidivism and considerably cost-effective compared to the costs of imprisonment. (Curtis, 1987a.)

What Do We Mean by Violence?

> *Violence is acting with intent to injure.*

In its simplest form, *violence is acting with intent to injure.* It suggests physical force but can also include other actions that hurt or injure in nonphysical ways such as verbal abuse or neglect. It also suggests the unlawful use of power or force—a behavior that is unjust.

Culturally, we sanction certain forms of violence. For example, some states permit capital punishment, and nations legitimize and promote killing in wartime. While these forms of violence may be morally debatable, the focus of this report is on individual acts of violence; violence that occurs between citizens of the same community or members of the same family.

For purposes of this discussion we will rely on the National Research Council (Reiss and Roth, editors) definition of violence: *behavior by persons against persons that intentionally threatens, attempts, or actually inflicts physical harm on others.*

---

[5] Minnesota Department of Planning (1995).

[6] Prentky and Burgess (1990) as quoted in Becker and Hunter Jr. (1992).

We chose this definition because most information collected about violent behavior, particularly information reported by law enforcement agencies and the criminal justice system, describes events that result or relate to the physical harm of a person. But this definition is somewhat limiting; it addresses neither the psychological and emotional aspects of violence nor the "abuse of power" concept that is important in describing family violence and child abuse.

Consider this broader definition of violence: *any action that is an abuse of power and where the intent is to control by causing pain, fear, or hurt; actions and words that hurt people.*

This definition includes the psychological harm and intimidation that accompanies many violent acts. Unfortunately, many elements of this broader definition are not easily tracked or quantifiable. That is because this society has developed ways of counting the number of broken bones, damaged houses, and bruises, but it is less adept at monitoring other dimensions of violence such as the psychological and emotional pain caused by violent behavior. Therefore, most indicators mentioned in this report describe the physical aspect of violence.

Types of Violence

While violence can be defined in broad or narrow terms, most violence that is measured has two characteristics: (1) it can be counted fairly readily, and (2) data collection is based on some federal, state, county, or community reporting requirement. Homicides, suicides, rapes and other forms of assault have these two characteristics. More recently, violent acts like domestic abuse, elder abuse, and bias crimes are being investigated and counted. Other forms of violence, like sexual harassment, chronic neglect, school bullying, and other behaviors that cause hurt without leaving physical bruises are coming under increasing scrutiny, but are not yet quantified adequately for us to include in this report.

Categories of Violent Acts Used in This Report

1. Assaultive violence
2. Child abuse
3. Rape and sexual assault
4. Domestic abuse
5. Elder abuse
6. Suicide
7. Bias (hate) crimes

In this report, we identify and organize seven categories of violent acts for which some prevalence information is available. The categories are assaultive violence, child abuse, rape and sexual assault, domestic abuse, elder abuse, suicide, and bias (hate) crimes. Legal definitions for these categories of violence vary from state to state and can even differ at the level of municipality. Our definitions are generalizations based on those used by various researchers. Further on in this report, we provide you with some guidelines for monitoring local violence using definitions consistent with the reporting requirements of your region. Our working definitions are as follows:

Assaultive Violence

Fatal and nonfatal interpersonal violence where physical force or other means is used by one person with the intent of causing harm, injury, or death to another (Rosenberg and Fenley, 1991).

Child Abuse and Child Sexual Abuse

1. The physical or mental injury, sexual abuse, negligent treatment, or maltreatment of a child under the age of eighteen by a person who is responsible for the child's welfare under circumstances which would indicate that the child's health or welfare is harmed or threatened (The Federal Child Abuse Prevention and Treatment Act of 1974).

2. Sexual contact with a child that occurs as a result of force in a relationship where it is exploitative because of an age difference or caretaking responsibility (Rosenberg and Fenley, 1991).

Rape and Sexual Assault

Nonconsensual oral, anal, or vaginal penetration obtained through the use of force or threat of force (Rosenberg and Fenley, 1991).

Domestic Abuse

The use of physical force in intimate relationships among adults (Rosenberg and Fenley, 1991).

Elder Abuse

An act of commission or omission that jeopardizes the well-being or safety of an elderly individual. The maltreatment of the elder may occur in the home and may include the following dimensions: physical abuse, emotional abuse, neglect or deprivation, material exploitation, sexual exploitation, and physical or verbal assault (Lucas, 1991).

Suicide

The act of taking one's own life voluntarily and intentionally (Webster's New Collegiate Dictionary, 1981).

Bias Crimes (Crimes Motivated by Racism, Sexism, or Bigotry)

Discrimination based on gender or race. Intolerance of another's religion, culture, party, sexual preference, opinion (Webster's New Collegiate Dictionary, 1981).

What Is a Rural Community?

In addition to defining what we mean by violence, we also must define "rural." There are many ways to define rural, most of which are complicated and confusing. In general, however, we have defined rural communities as communities that are not part of metropolitan statistical areas and contain less than 25,000 people.

When reporting statistics, however, we have used the specific definitions of rural that have been used by the reporting agencies. Those references and definitions are noted in the text.

How Can This Book Be Helpful?

All too often our confrontations with violence leave us frustrated and angry. Because of its many forms and its association with momentary and intense emotion, controlling violent behavior appears to be difficult, if not impossible.

Yet, there are things that can be done and are being done now in small communities throughout America to:

- Reduce the likelihood that conflicts escalate to violence.

- Increase the safety of public areas.

- Identify and reduce the social conditions which help to breed violence.

- Help mothers and fathers learn parenting practices that instill nonviolent behaviors in children.

- Help people to escape from abusive partners.

- Help victims of violence to recover.

- Help perpetrators of violence to reduce their violent acts.

- Restore a sense of justice when violence has occurred.

This report describes an approach residents of any community can use to become aware of violence in their own communities, identify target areas for reducing violence, monitor community trends related to violence, and begin to see differences in their community's level of violence.

Use Section One, Strategies to Reduce Violence, to gain an overview of the kinds of strategies that may reduce specific types of violence. The strategies are listed according to the research information available about their effectiveness, so you can make some judgment as to a specific strategy's potential in your community. Those strategies which have been applied and studied in rural areas are noted, and we have summarized those violence prevention programs that, while implemented in urban communities, also show promise in rural communities. Most strategies listed in Section One are followed by a reference number indicating a brief summation of the strategy in Appendix A, Literature Review Matrix. If you choose a specific strategy for your community, we suggest you turn to the original research to be found through the Bibliography.

Use Section Two, Community Report Card, to begin the process of collecting and recording the levels of violence and violence-related services in your community. The report card section provides a step-by-step description of how to collect, record, and use information about community risk factors related to violence and violent events. We have provided worksheets, which you can reproduce as needed, to facilitate your work. ■

What strategies are most likely to reduce violence in your community? We surveyed the research on techniques to prevent and reduce violence, as well as methods to heal the damage caused by violence. This report contains those strategies shown to be mildly to strongly successful, as well as those that multiple experts believe will be successful, but which have not been formally researched.

Note that not all strategies currently in use are reported here. This is because many such strategies simply haven't been documented in the literature.

Certain strategies cut across all types of violence. For example, alcohol and other drug abuse are linked to most types of violence, so a strategy aimed at reducing such abuse would apply to most types of violence. These strategies are listed in this section under *Strategies That Cut across All Categories of Violence,* pages 10-13.

Other strategies work within a specific category of violence. These are listed in this section under *Strategies for Specific Types of Violence*, pages 14-26.

In both of these strategy segments, reference numbers are provided so you can read about the specific strategy in Appendix A: Literature Review Matrix, pages 47-69.

How to Use This Information

You can use this information to help you select strategies that best fit your community. *All* of these strategies are believed to be or known to be useful. The more you know about the kinds of violence and the scope of the problems, the better you will be able to choose strategies that are appropriate. Here are some things to consider as you select strategies:

The Type of Violence

Some types of strategies seem to work best for particular kinds of violence. For example, couples counseling is not effective for domestic abuse but may be helpful in the area of child maltreatment.

The Scope of the Problem

Is there a widespread problem across the community or is it focused in one geographical location or within one population group? For example, if there is a problem of sexual harassment in the high school, it may make sense to use an educational strategy with the affected population. If sexual harassment is occurring at all levels of the community, a more broad-based strategy (or multiple strategies) may be called for.

The Resources Available

Does the community have the resources to implement the particular strategy you are considering? For example, a large-scale poverty reduction strategy may require more resources than your community has available. A home visiting program with low-income families might be less costly but still helpful.

The Needs and Interests of the Community

Strategies that don't fit the culture and interests of the community—that is, strategies that don't receive broad support—are not as likely to succeed. For example, in considering a strategy to reduce violence linked to substance abuse, you would ask, Does the community have a strong interest in having substance abuse treatment programs more widely available? Is there motivation among treatment professionals to collaborate more closely? The strategy will be more successful if the community and its residents are predisposed to take the actions required by the strategy.

Strategies That Cut across All Categories of Violence

- Reduction of Alcohol and Other Drug Abuse
- Education and Cross-discipline Collaboration
- Reduction of Poverty
- The Availability of Safe Places
- The Availability of Health Care for Women and Mental Health and Supportive Services for All
- Restrict Access to Firearms

Strategies That Cut across All Categories of Violence

Certain strategies impact *all* types of violence. These broad-based strategies, listed below, influence most types of violent behavior and its consequences. They are not ranked according to their level of importance or effectiveness.

Reduction of Alcohol and Other Drug Abuse

Alcohol and other drug abuse is highly associated with many types of violent behavior. Reducing the abuse of alcohol and other drugs helps reduce violence in a variety of ways.

- Alcohol and other drugs have a disinhibiting effect upon some people and may precipitate aggression. Reduction in use, therefore, may reduce violent behavior.

- The illegal drug market accounts for violence in many communities. Thus violence may be reduced by reducing demand or legalizing drugs.

- Children born to alcohol and drug abusing mothers tend to have problems such as cognitive deficits and hyperactivity, which are precursors to violent behavior.

- Communities can make treatment available for drug and alcohol abuse. Education and prevention programs for children have shown success in delaying the age at which youth begin using drugs and alcohol.

- Adding taxes to the sale of alcohol has resulted in a reduction in auto fatalities when done on a state level, but no studies of this have been conducted at the community level.

For more information on these strategies, see A-8, A-25, D-15, F-8.

Education and Cross-discipline Collaboration

Collaboration among agencies providing services to victims, offenders, and the community around issues of violence helps provide efficient services to all groups. This includes collaboration among medical personnel, legal services, criminal justice, police schools, victim's advocates, child protection agencies, social services, and so forth. Collaboration and education impact violence in the following ways:

- Agency cooperation has led to better identification and quicker, more effective referrals.

- Collaboration between agencies has reduced the re-victimization of victims, particularly in cases of child abuse, and has led to better prosecution of offenders.

- Agency cooperation is critical in getting needed services to victims of elder abuse.

- Education of service providers, teachers, medical personnel, and social services staff has been shown to be important in helping to identify victims, in providing victims with more control, and in gathering evidence for prosecution.

For more information on these strategies, see B_1-8, B_1-10, B_1-11, B_1-14, B_2-2, C-4, C-5, D-3, D-7, E-3, E-4.

Reduction of Poverty

Violence occurs in families and communities of all economic circumstances. However, conditions associated with poverty, such as family disruption, poor access to prenatal and child care, and low birth weight are all associated with both aggressive violent behavior and child abuse and neglect. Lack of jobs, particularly for young people, has been linked to the development of gangs. There are no studies directly linking reduction of poverty and reduced violent behavior, but communities that have less poverty have lower incidence of violent acts.

For more information on this strategy, see A-13.

The Availability of Safe Places

The availability of safe houses and shelters for victims of violence helps alleviate or reduce violence, at least for that period of time the victim is away from the offender. Shelters or safe houses for battered women and their children, safe houses for teens, and crisis nurseries for children have been the most common form of safe places. In Europe, some communities also have shelters for elderly victims of abuse.

For more information on this strategy, see B_1-12, B_1-15, D-9, E-9.

The Availability of Health Care for Women and Mental Health and Supportive Services for All

Increasing the availability of prenatal and postnatal health care for women has not traditionally been thought of as a violence prevention strategy. However, some causes of violent behavior in individuals can be traced back to poor prenatal and postnatal care of the mother.

- Exposure to drugs, alcohol, and lead results in premature birth or low birth weight. These substances cause disabilities and deficits in children that lead to lack of problem-solving ability, low intelligence, and aggressive behavior, all of which are directly linked to criminal and violent behavior.

For more information on this strategy see A-6, B_1-13.

- Health care services, mental health services, support groups, and crisis lines have shown to be helpful, and at times, essential to the recovery of victims.

For more information on this strategy, see A-16, B_1-2, B_1-16, B_2-3, C-6, C-8, D-4, D-8, E-5, E-6, F-2, F-6, F-10.

Restrict Access to Firearms

Research has not shown that gun availability causes violent acts. However, violent acts involving guns are generally more lethal than those that do not involve guns. Evidence shows that reduced access to guns in a community can reduce the number of suicides, homicides, and robberies using guns. Enacting laws that increase jail sentences for crime using guns have reduced the harm done from gun violence; in states where a one-year mandated sentence was added to the convicted person's sentence, gun use decreased in assaults, robberies, and homicides.

For more information on this strategy, see A-10, F-3.

Summary

Efforts to make a difference across all categories of violence include reducing drug and alcohol abuse, increasing community collaboration and education, reducing poverty, increasing the availability of health care and safe places for victims, and restricting access to firearms. Most of these efforts require a strong commitment as well as support programs and policies that cut across a number of service areas and political arenas. The final outcome may be a stronger impact on reducing violent behavior, providing help for victims, and reducing offender recidivism. ■

Strategies for Specific Types of Violence

Following is a list of strategies that impact specific types of violence. To help you explore which of these strategies might best suit your community, we have divided them into four categories, described below. Please note that these categories are *not* a rating of the potential impact of the strategy in a given situation—that is, don't interpret the category to mean that one strategy is better than another. Rather, the rating tells you what kind of research was conducted on the strategy.

1. *Strategies that show substantial evidence of effectiveness in reducing violence or victim trauma.* These are strategies that have been evaluated using controlled experimental research designs, and that show substantial evidence of reducing violence or reducing the trauma to victims. Experimental research designs that include a control group can show more definitively whether the strategy has made a difference in reducing violence.

   Consider this example:

   Residents in a community decide to implement a schoolwide intervention to reduce bullying. After a year, the number of fights in school decreases, the number of school suspensions due to fighting are reduced, and students and teachers feel more comfortable and safe at school. It is not possible to know whether those changes occurred because of the activities of the school intervention or because of other factors such as changes in the school population, economic conditions of the community, changes in school policies, or any number of other factors. Comparing the students involved in the schoolwide intervention with other similar students not involved in the intervention activities (called the control group) would indicate the probability that the strategy actually made the difference in how people behaved. If the number of fights, school suspensions, and so forth in the control group did not change, then the experiment supports the conclusion that the strategy caused the change rather than some other factor.

2. *Strategies that show moderate evidence of effectiveness.* The strategies in this category have been evaluated using study methods that did not include a control group. Such studies may have included pretests and posttests, follow-up surveys, or other evaluative methods. These strategies show promise of preventing violence or reducing victim trauma, yet it is unclear how strong the connection is between the strategy and the reduction in violent behavior.

3. *Strategies that attempt to change intermediary factors that influence violent behavior and associated trauma.* These strategies focus on changing the knowledge, attitudes, and skills of either offenders or potential victims of violence. In any circumstance of potential conflict, the escalation to violence is in part related to the attitudes, knowledge, and skills of those involved. One strategy to reduce the potential for violence is to develop programs and services that influence the attitudes, knowledge, and skills a person has for resolving conflict. Such strategies may benefit potential victims by increasing their ability to assess dangerous situations, find help, or cope with uncomfortable feelings. These strategies have not been proven effective in reducing violence per se. Rather, they have been shown to influence the attitudes, knowledge, and skills of those involved in conflicts or those who may be victims of violence. The assumption is that therefore, the level of violence or trauma will be reduced.

4. *Strategies proposed by experts to reduce violence and help victims of trauma.* Strategies in this category are ones that a number of experts believe to be helpful but that have not been systematically evaluated. These strategies may influence factors that are strongly associated with violent behavior, such as poverty and substance abuse.

Most of the studies we reviewed were not specific to rural communities; there simply is a shortage of such studies. We have made a special notation for those strategies that have shown evidence of effectiveness in rural communities. Such studies have the icon ✪ placed next to them.

Assaultive Violence

Summary   The research indicates that to reduce assaultive violence, it is important to start when people are young. Efforts to help children become less violent by teaching them problem-solving techniques and cognitive skills have shown success, as have efforts to reduce violence in elementary schools. Experts believe, and evidence exists, that improving conditions such as poverty, poor prenatal care, school failure, and substance abuse will reduce violent behavior. Limiting access to firearms may reduce the severity of injuries and result in fewer homicides and suicides, but does not reduce the occurrences of violent behavior in general.

Victim-offender mediation programs show success in helping victims regain a sense of control. Victim assistance services are believed to be helpful, but no research has been conducted to confirm this. Services for victims such as health care, mental health services, legal services, and so forth, help victims recover.

Incarceration of offenders without rehabilitative services has no effect upon recidivism. Rehabilitative services, treatment programs, and community-based programs all show some level of effectiveness with some offenders. Programs are less effective with the most violent offenders. Victim-offender mediation programs have shown success in reducing recidivism with young offenders.

Assaultive Violence Strategies	Substantial evidence of effectiveness	Moderate evidence of effectiveness	Evidence of effective intermediary strategy	No research, but strategy proposed by multiple experts	Evidence of effectiveness in rural areas
Prevention and Intervention Strategies					
Reducing school failure (A-7)	✔				✪
Restrict access to firearms (A-10)	✔				✪
Schoolwide interventions to reduce bullying (A-1)	✔				✪
Delinquency prevention programs (A-4)			✔		
Education about diverse groups of people (A-3)			✔		
Teaching conflict resolution and problem-solving skills (A-2)			✔		✪
Neighborhood mediation centers (A-12)			✔		
Increase the availability of prenatal and postnatal care (A-6)				✔	✪
Reduce substance abuse (A-8)				✔	
Reduce poverty (A-13)				✔	
Services for Victims					
Victim-offender mediation (A-15)		✔			✪
Trauma and health services for victims (A-16)				✔	
Victim assistance services (A-14)				✔	
Offender Services to Reduce Recidivism					
Incarceration with rehabilitation for adults and juveniles (A-19)	✔				
Restitution for juvenile offenders (A-21)	✔				
Halfway houses and reentry programs (A-24)		✔			
Victim-offender mediation (A-26)		✔			✪
Social skills interventions for children (A-17)		✔			
Swift arrest and prosecution (A-23)				✔	
Alcohol and drug abuse treatment (A-25)				✔	

Child Abuse and Child Sexual Abuse

Summary   Parenting support and education have helped reduce child maltreatment. For families with a greater risk of child abuse and child sexual abuse, comprehensive services, which may include intensive case management and home visits, have been effective in both rural and urban settings. The use of trained volunteers and paraprofessionals has been a good strategy, particularly in rural communities.

In many communities, agencies cooperate across disciplines to manage cases, work with victims, and prosecute offenders. Mental health services help victims cope with symptoms related to abuse. Shelters, crisis nurseries, and foster care have stopped the abuse, at least for the period of time the child is away from the abuser.

The combination of therapeutic support and basic care services has reduced maltreatment in some families. There is no effective treatment for chronic child abusers.

Child Abuse and Child Sexual Abuse Strategies

	Substantial evidence of effectiveness	Moderate evidence of effectiveness	Evidence of effective intermediary strategy	No research, but strategy proposed by multiple experts	Evidence of effectiveness in rural areas
Prevention and Intervention Strategies					
Comprehensive home visiting child abuse services (B_1-5)	✔				⊛
Mental health services (B_1-9)		✔			
Child-targeted sexual abuse prevention programs (B_2-1)			✔		⊛
Parenting support and education (B_1-3)			✔		
Use of lay and paraprofessional helpers to provide parenting support and education (B_1-6)			✔		⊛
Education and training for professionals working with children (B_2-2)			✔		
Prenatal and postnatal health care (B_1-1)				✔	⊛
Education and public awareness (B_1-7)				✔	⊛
Interdisciplinary cooperation between agencies working with families (B_1-11)				✔	
Services for Victims					
Model protocols in health clinics and hospitals (B_1-8)		✔			
Mental health services (B_1-9, B_2-3)		✔			
Foster care/shelters (B_1-15)		✔			⊛
Therapeutic day care (B_1-12)		✔			
Criminal justice reforms such as guardians ad litem, victim assistance, reduced number of interviews, children's centers (B_1-13, B_1-14)				✔	
Offender Services to Reduce Recidivism					
Therapeutic support for families (B_1-16)		✔			
Juvenile sex offender treatment (B_2-5)		✔			⊛
Adult sex offender treatment (B_2-7)		✔			
Criminal sanctions (B_2-6)				✔	
Substance abuse treatment (B_1-17)				✔	

Rape and Sexual Assault

Summary   Public education and awareness programs have changed attitudes about rape and sexual assault. However, it is not known whether such programs actually change behavior.

The development of model protocols and the instruction of emergency room personnel to use those protocols have been successful in identifying victims and gathering evidence for prosecution. Mental health services for victims and their families have reduced the stress and depression associated with assaults. Victim support services and the advocacy associated with those services are believed to be useful.

Swift arrest and prosecution show some evidence of reducing repeat offenses. Specialized sex offender treatment programs that include cognitive, behavioral, and group therapy show some evidence of effectiveness with some offenders. In many studies, sex offenders were frequently found to have histories of physical or sexual abuse. Most adult sex offenders started their offense history during adolescence. Focusing efforts on young sex offenders may prove to be the most effective way to prevent future cases. Early treatment of young sex offenders appears to be effective. Chronic offenders have not been treated effectively in these programs.

Rape and Sexual Assault Strategies

	Substantial evidence of effectiveness	Moderate evidence of effectiveness	Evidence of effective intermediary strategy	No research, but strategy proposed by multiple experts	Evidence of effectiveness in rural areas
Prevention and Intervention Strategies					
Education and raising awareness (C-1)			✔		
Treatment of adolescent sex offenders (C-7)			✔		
Reduction in pornography (C-2)				✔	
Services for Victims					
Mental health and support services (C-8)			✔		
Crisis lines (C-6)			✔		✪
Advocacy (C-9)				✔	
Establish model protocols in hospitals (C-4)				✔	
Cooperation among agencies (C-5)				✔	✪
Victim-offender mediation (C-10)				✔	
Offender Services to Reduce Recidivism					
Specialized treatment programs, including drug therapy (C-12, C-13)	✔				✪
Swift arrest and prosecution (C-11)				✔	

Domestic Abuse

Summary Public education and awareness programs have been shown to increase positive attitudes toward nonviolence and have encouraged individuals to report domestic abuse, but no studies have shown changes in behavior as a result of such programs.

Crisis telephone services are particularly important in rural areas to link women with supportive services. Orders for protection have reduced violence in less severe offenders in some cases, and shelters have reduced family violence. Cooperation among agencies that work with families and the establishment of medical protocols to help doctors identify and work with victims are believed to be helpful in identifying victims and providing services to them. Conflict resolution programs are believed to reduce domestic abuse, but the effectiveness of these programs has not been studied. The use of citizen and police intervention teams has reduced family violence in both urban and rural environments. Mental health services have reduced depression in victims. Advocacy and victim assistance services are believed to be helpful in providing both emotional support and encouraging victims to take effective legal action.

Domestic Abuse Strategies	Substantial evidence of effectiveness	Moderate evidence of effectiveness	Evidence of effective intermediary strategy	No research, but strategy proposed by multiple experts	Evidence of effectiveness in rural areas
Prevention and Intervention Strategies					
Police and citizen intervention teams (D-6)		✔			✪
Education and public awareness (D-1, D-2)			✔		
Cooperation among agencies (D-3)				✔	✪
Conflict resolution programs (D-5)				✔	
Services for Victims					
Safe houses or shelters (D-9)	✔				✪
Orders for protection (D-12)	✔				
Therapy and mental health services (D-8)		✔			✪
Crisis lines (D-4)		✔			
Establish protocols in health settings to identify and refer victims (D-7)				✔	
Advocacy and victim assistance services (D-10, D-11)				✔	
Offender Services to Reduce Recidivism					
Swift arrest and mandated treatment (D-13, D-14)	✔				
Spouse abuse treatment programs (D-16, D-18)		✔			
Substance abuse treatment (D-15)				✔	
Self-help groups (D-17)				✔	

Elder Abuse

Summary   Reducing the isolation of older people in their families and educating the public about the aging process are believed to prevent elder abuse.

Protocols for identifying and working with victims in hospitals and doctors' offices have raised awareness about and increased referral of victims. Crisis telephone services have been successful in linking isolated elderly to needed services. Experts believe the cooperation of agencies working with families is essential in providing the wide range of services needed. Emergency shelters and foster care are believed to be helpful to victims.

Experts believe reducing the level of dependency between the victim and the offender through comprehensive services is the most effective treatment.

Elder Abuse Strategies

	Substantial evidence of effectiveness	Moderate evidence of effectiveness	Evidence of effective intermediary strategy	No research, but strategy proposed by multiple experts	Evidence of effectiveness in rural areas
Prevention and Intervention Strategies					
Public awareness and education (E-2)			✔		
Model protocols in health settings (E-3)			✔		
Cooperation among agencies (E-4)			✔		
Reduce social isolation in families (E-1)				✔	
Crisis telephone services (E-5)				✔	
Services for Victims					
Mental health services (E-6)	✔				
Community supports (home visits, day care, and respite) (E-7)				✔	
Emergency shelters (E-9)				✔	
Case management (E-8)				✔	
Offender Services to Reduce Recidivism					
Comprehensive services (education, counseling, employment, homemaker, self-sufficiency, and support) (E-10)				✔	

Suicide

Effective ways to prevent suicide include educating people about the topic, making mental health services accessible, and limiting access to common means used in suicide such as guns and high places.

Summary

Mental health services are effective in suicide intervention. Community intervention teams used in rural areas have helped survivors cope and prevented repeat suicide attempts. Walk-in counseling centers and crisis telephone services are believed to be helpful, but their effectiveness is difficult to assess because follow-up data is hard to collect.

Mental health services are effective in helping to reduce the stresses that may precipitate suicide. Informal support and trained volunteers have been shown to be helpful ways to deliver services in rural communities.

Suicide Reduction Strategies

	Substantial evidence of effectiveness	Moderate evidence of effectiveness	Evidence of effective intermediary strategy	No research, but strategy proposed by multiple experts	Evidence of effectiveness in rural areas
Prevention and Intervention Strategies					
Limit access to common means of suicide (guns, high places) (F-3)	✔				
Mental health and supportive services (self-help groups, peer counselors, treatment for depression) (F-10)		✔			✪
Crisis services (F-4, F-6)		✔			
Education and increasing awareness (F-1, F-5)			✔		
Community intervention teams (F-7)				✔	
Substance abuse treatment (F-8)				✔	

Bias Crimes

Summary   Efforts to reduce racism, sexism, and bigotry in communities include educational programs on diversity in schools and the workplace, religious initiatives against racism, and broad-based community actions. All are believed to be helpful, but there are no studies of effectiveness.

Mediation programs in urban communities have been successful in reducing violence and developing better understanding between people.

Criminal sanctions against people who commit hate crimes is believed to be a deterrent.

Bias Crime Strategies	Substantial evidence of effectiveness	Moderate evidence of effectiveness	Evidence of effective intermediary strategy	No research, but strategy proposed by multiple experts	Evidence of effectiveness in rural areas
Prevention and Intervention Strategies					
Mediation programs (G-5)			✔		
Conflict resolution training programs (G-6)			✔		
Diversity training (G-1)				✔	
Cooperative learning (G-2)				✔	
Religious initiatives against racism (G-3)				✔	
Broad-based community efforts (G-4)				✔	
Services for Victims					
Advocacy (G-7)		✔			
Offender Services to Reduce Recidivism					
Hate crimes bill/criminal sanctions (G-8)				✔	

Lessons from Urban Community Violence Reduction Programs

Violence prevention programs have been implemented in many urban communities in the last decade and show promise in reducing violent activities and crime. The characteristics of those successful programs may have applicability to violence in rural communities.

The following is a synthesis of the findings from the Eisenhower Foundation National Neighborhood Program and the Violent Juvenile Offender Research and Development Program. Both were community development oriented, violence prevention programs. They served youth in a total of sixteen urban communities (Curtis, 87; Fagan, 87).

- Programs were led by community groups and members rather than by the police or criminal justice system.

- Programs targeted youth and high risk young adults but also included families.

- Program components included neighborhood, family, and school mediation, drug counseling, recreation and arts, youth employment counseling and tutoring, community organizing, street patrols, victim and witness assistance and advocacy, and family support.

- Outcomes included an actual reduction in reported crime in one site, less drug use and criminal activity for the youth directly involved in programs, a reduction of fear in the community, improved job skills, and development of neighborhood leadership skills.

- Both demonstrations incorporated a needs assessment to determine the community's most pressing problems and to uncover those goals most desired by the community.

- Both demonstrations reported needing additional time to have an effect on violence indicators.

- Cooperation from local institutions such as schools, police, courts, and child protection was not always forthcoming, although it was necessary to accomplish the goals. ■

Community
Report
Card

How can your community measure its current levels of violence? How can you know if your community has the resources to help victims? What can your community do to monitor violence and perhaps prevent violence from occurring in the first place?

After we reviewed the literature on violence, we set about to create a tool with which communities could assess their current situation and choose strategies to respond to violence. The result is the following *Community Report Card.* The Community Report Card helps communities examine various risk factors, indicators of violence, and resources for victim assistance and violence prevention.

We know, from the research, that violence is linked to other conditions in the community. These conditions include community composition, economic stress, educational attainment, health, and alcohol and other drug use. Because these factors are all linked to the risk of violence, the community needs to begin by forming an accurate picture of its status within each of these categories. Thus Part 1 of the Community Report Card, Community Risk Factors, asks you to collect information on these risk factors. Later, as you develop strategies to respond to violence, you can use this information in several ways. It may help you form a hypothesis about the underlying causes of violence in your community. It may help you select a broad-based strategy to impact many forms of violence at once. It may help you understand the kinds of public awareness efforts you'll need to undertake. Or it may help you anticipate the way your community will respond to a proposed strategy.

> **Community Conditions
> Linked to Risk of Violence**
>
> - Community Composition
> - Economic Stress
> - Educational Attainment
> - Health
> - Alcohol and Other Drug Use

The next step is to understand the types and amount of violence your community is experiencing. Here, Part 2 of the Community Report Card, Violent Events, asks you to collect data on specific violent events, including assaultive violence, domestic abuse, rape and sexual assault, bias crimes, child abuse, elder abuse, and suicide. Such numbers can dispel sensational news coverage, illuminate patterns that otherwise are not apparent, and help your community decide which forms of violence to address.

You also need an accurate picture of how your community currently responds to violence. Therefore, Part 3 of the Community Report Card, Service Availability and Accessibility, includes a number of questions about the types of services available in your community, as well as their accessibility. Here, you may discover gaping holes in service, opportunities for collaboration between service providers, resources you were unaware of, and possible "paths of least resistance" for changes you wish to initiate.

The final step in preparing the Community Report Card is to put the data in a format that gives you some perspective. We have created two worksheets to help you do this. Part 4a: Community Comparisons (page 45) provides space for you to compare your community with another community or with your county. You may wish to share your data with a similar size community, follow the trends, and thus gain some sense of how your efforts are succeeding (or not) in comparison with another community. Part 4b: Comparisons over Time (page 46) allows you to compile the individual data on risk factors and violent events on one page, which you can repeat annually to develop a long-term view of violence in your community.

Using the Report Card Worksheets

Each of the worksheets that make up the Community Report Card is accompanied by a brief note explaining why the information is important and how to collect it. Unfortunately, there is no single source for the data you'll need to collect; you will have to track down as much of the information as you can by turning to a variety of sources, ranging from state offices to the local school district. To help you get started, we have provided the most generic source for the information. For each community there may be a local office that provides the information needed. For example, U.S. Census information or population estimates can be acquired through state, county, or city planning agencies; health information is available through county or city public health offices; crime information is available through the local police or sheriff's department.

After you have collected the data on risk factors, violent events, and services, you can compile the data on the Community Report Card worksheet itself. This is the baseline data you'll want to track from year to year, and compare with other communities.

Part 1: Community Risk Factors

What is your community's risk of violence? You can begin to answer this question by looking at your community's size and composition, economic health, educational attainment, physical health, and use of alcohol and other drugs. As you collect answers to the questions that follow, fill them in on the Risk Factors worksheet on page 41.

Community Composition

To assess the risk of violence occurring in your community, it is important to know about the types of people who live there. In general, the larger the population in the community, the higher the rate of violent crime (NRC, Reiss and Roth, eds.). Teenagers and young adult males tend to be both the perpetrators and the victims of violent crimes (U.S. Department of Justice, 1992; Reiss and Roth, 1993). A community with a large number of males between the ages of fifteen and thirty is likely to have higher violent crime rates than a community that has fewer males in that age category. The risk of being a victim of violent crime for different races in rural communities is debatable. Whites tend to have higher victimization rates in rural areas, while in suburbs and cities, Blacks are more at risk of being victimized (U.S. Department of Justice, 1992). However, in a study of violent crime in Minnesota high schools, Native American students in rural communities report being victimized more often than White students in rural Minnesota (Higgins, 1994). Whether ethnic or racial status puts a person at more or less risk in rural communities is unclear and may differ by community or population. However, the racial and ethnic composition of a community is still an important consideration.

Population

Community size influences its character, and data on population will give you a baseline from which to work. In general, the larger the population, the greater the crime rate (U.S. Department of Justice, 1992).

Rationale

Information on community composition is in the 1990 U.S. Census. You can also check with the State Demographer's Office or the city or county planning office for population estimates.

Finding information

Fill in this number on line one of the Risk Factors worksheet.

Age

Rationale Young people between the ages of fifteen and twenty-four are more likely to be perpetrators and victims of violent crime (Reiss and Roth, eds., 1993; U.S. Department of Justice, 1992).

Finding information The U.S. Census provides information on the age distribution of the population in a community. The local city or planning department may have estimates.

Fill in the number of people in each age category on lines two through seven of the Risk Factors worksheet. To compute the percentage of each age group as part of the total population, divide the number for that age group by the total population of the community. Multiply that number by one hundred and record it as a percent.

Diversity

Rationale While diversity enriches a community's cultural resources, diversity brings a difference in beliefs and values that may heighten conflict. The more diverse the community, the more skills the population needs to address the numerous and sometimes conflicting desires of the various groups.

Finding information The U.S. Census provides information about the racial and ethnic composition of the community. Religious affiliation can be counted by contacting the local places of worship.

Fill in the number of people in each ethnic, racial, and religious group on lines eight through fifteen of the Risk Factors worksheet; add other lines as needed. To compute the percentage of each group as a part of the total population, divide that group's population by the total community population. Multiply that number by one hundred and record it as a percent.

Economic Stress

High rates of poverty are consistently linked with high rates of violence. Children from low income homes are at a higher risk of injury due to abuse and neglect. Poverty and unemployment reflect a lack of economic opportunity in the community. Other factors related to community poverty also influence crime and violence, such as feelings of persistent powerlessness, school failure, lack of constructive recreational activities for youth, lack of medical and child care, and high levels of family disruption. In this report card, we suggest measuring economic stress by examining single parent families, poverty, unemployment, and educational attainment (Reiss and Roth, 1993).

Percent of Single Parent Families

Single parent families, usually headed by a female, tend to have lower incomes than two parent families. Single parent households show a pattern of family disruption in the community which affects the community's ability to supervise young males (Reiss and Roth, 1993).

Rationale

This indicator can be found in the 1990 U.S. Census. City or county planning boards may have up-to-date estimates. The local school planning offices may also have this information.

Finding information

Record the percent of single parent families on line sixteen of the Risk Factors worksheet.

Percent Below Poverty

The percent below poverty is an indicator of economic stress.

Rationale

This indicator can be found in the 1990 U.S. Census and some state or regional economic development reports. To find the percent below poverty, divide the number of people living below the poverty line by the total number of people in your community. Multiply this number by one hundred and record it as a percent.

Finding information

Fill in the number and percent of people living below poverty on line seventeen of the Risk Factors worksheet.

Percent Unemployment (among people age sixteen and older)

This indicator represents the percent of employable people who are not working, which is another indicator of poverty.

Rationale

For the most up-to-date information, contact the local or regional planning department, or the state department of economic development. This statistic is usually given as a percentage.

Finding information

Fill in the percent of unemployment on line eighteen of the Risk Factors worksheet.

Educational Attainment

Percent of Adults with High School Diploma (age twenty-five and over)

Rationale Adult violent offenders tend to have low IQ and a history of school failure (Reiss and Roth, 1993). The most often used measure of educational attainment is the percentage of adults (age twenty-five and over) who have earned their high school diploma or the equivalent. Access to employment options is determined, in part, by the education of the individual who is seeking employment. Lack of a high school diploma limits work opportunities.

Finding information The level of educational attainment for the community can be found using the U.S. Census, which lists the number of adults over age twenty-five with a high school diploma or its equivalent. Divide this number by the total population over age twenty-five and multiply by one hundred to compute the percentage of adults with a high school diploma.

Fill in the number and percent of adults with a high school diploma on line nineteen of the Risk Factors worksheet.

School Attendance and Dropout Rates

Rationale A good predictor of success in school is the attendance in previous years. Therefore, attendance records can be used as an early indication of children who might be at risk of dropping out. Success in school is linked to literacy and employment opportunities.

Finding information Contact the local school district. School records will provide attendance data and dropout rates.

Attendance data is reported differently in each district and state. Fill in the number from your local school district for school attendance on line twenty and the number and percent of dropouts on line twenty-one of the Risk Factors worksheet.

Health

Researchers have identified some antecedents of aggressive childhood behavior which can lead to violent behavior as adults. Those factors include low birth weight babies and babies whose mothers have had pregnancy and birth complications (Reiss and Roth, 1993). Mothers without adequate support, parenting skills and experience, and maturity are at an increased risk of abusing their children (Connelly and Straus, 1992).

Low Birth Weight Babies

Low birth weight can be the result of lack of prenatal care, poor maternal nutrition or health, maternal substance abuse, premature delivery, or other problems. Low birth weight babies are more likely to experience speech, language, motor skill, and cognitive problems. Children with low cognitive functioning may be less able to work through conflict in a nonabusive manner.

Rationale

Birth weight is recorded on the birth certificate and is recorded and tracked by the Department of Health in most states. Low birth weight babies (less than 2,500 grams) are tracked as a percent of the total number of babies.

Finding information

Record the number and percent of low birth weight babies born in your area on line twenty-two of the Risk Factors worksheet.

Percent of Mothers under Age Eighteen

Young mothers are at risk of perpetrating child abuse, not because they are young but because of characteristics associated with early childbearing that are also associated with increased risk, such as single parenthood, inadequate support systems, insufficient knowledge of and experience in child rearing, inadequate education, poverty, immaturity, marital violence, and use of physical punishment (Connelly and Straus, 1992).

Rationale

Percent of mothers under eighteen can be found at the State Health Department, and may also be available from the local health department.

Finding information

Record the percent of mothers under age eighteen on line twenty-three of the Risk Factors worksheet.

Alcohol and Other Drug Use

Alcohol and other drug use are strong indicators of the risk of violence, as Jeffrey Roth reports in a 1994 U.S. Department of Justice Newsletter:

> *"Research has found strong correlations between violence and alcohol and other substance abuse. Research studies over the last several decades have shown that alcohol drinking by the perpetrator of a crime, the victim, or both has immediately preceded at least half of all violent events including murders. Chronic drinkers are more likely than other people to have histories of violent behavior. Criminals who use illegal drugs commit robberies and assaults more frequently than do non-user criminals, and they commit them especially frequently during periods of heavy drug use. Expectant mothers' alcohol and substance abuse during pregnancy adversely affects fetal development. The resultant damage causes learning problems that in turn increase the risk of early grade school failure."*

Driving under the Influence

Rationale   A high number of DUI's, as compared with other similar communities, may be indicative of a problem with substance abuse in the community. It may also mean there is better surveillance in the community with the higher rate: more people are getting caught.

Finding information   The local police or sheriff's department has information about driving under the influence of drugs or alcohol. This information is tracked on a statewide basis in some states. The information would be reported to the State Department of Public Safety or to the person in the state who organizes the uniform crime reports. The data may be reported as a number or a rate. The rate is the number of offenses divided by the population. To compute separate DUI rates for teens and adults, divide the number of teen offenses by the number of teenagers (ages sixteen to nineteen) in the population. For adults, divide the number of adult offenses by the number of adults in the population (ages nineteen and older). Multiply by 1,000 to get a rate per 1,000.

Record the information on lines twenty-four and twenty-five of the Risk Factors worksheet.

Narcotic Crime Reports

Rationale   Violence in many communities is associated with the illegal drug market (Roth, 1994).

Finding information   Contact the local police or sheriff's department or the State Department of Public Safety. This category of information generally includes all arrests for violations of state and local ordinances relating to unlawful possession, sale, use, growing, and manufacturing of narcotic drugs.

Record the information as a rate per 1,000 people: Divide the number of offenses by the total population, and multiply by 1,000. Record the information on line twenty-six of the Risk Factors worksheet.

Adolescent Alcohol Use

Rationale   Patterns of aggressive behavior and substance abuse often become intertwined starting in childhood. Aggressive childhood behavior is predictive of later heavy drinking, both of which are associated with an above average risk of adult violent behavior (Roth, 1994).

Finding information   The local police record the number of teens charged with underage drinking.

Record the number and percent on line twenty-seven of the Risk Factors worksheet.

Part 2: Violent Events

You can get a snapshot of violence in your community by collecting information on assaultive violence, domestic abuse, rape and sexual assault, bias crimes, suicide, elder abuse, and child abuse.

Assaultive Violence, Domestic Abuse, Rape and Sexual Assault, and Bias Crimes

Information on violent events such as assaults, domestic abuse, and rape and sexual assault is kept by local police and sheriff's departments. Often these crimes go unreported, particularly crimes involving family members and acquaintances. However, this is the most effective and least costly way to acquire information on violent events. Definitions of violent crimes vary by state. Check your state laws for specific definitions.

Background

Contact the local police or sheriff's department or the State Department of Public Safety. Most communities provide yearly reports of this information. If you work closely with your sources you may be able to get the information more often, perhaps quarterly. Local schools may keep records on the numbers of students suspended or expelled for fighting and the incidences of sexual harassment.

Finding information

Record the information on lines one through seventeen of the Violent Events worksheet as number of occurrences and rates per 1,000 people. If available, record the number of adult and juvenile offenders, and any information on the use of weapons.

Child Abuse and Elder Abuse

Child abuse is reported as child physical abuse, child sexual abuse, child emotional abuse, or neglect. On this report card, you can record three types of reports:

Background

1. Substantiated abuse: abuse that was proven to have occurred.

2. Unsubstantiated report: abuse that was investigated and found not to have occurred.

3. Unable to substantiate: abuse that was investigated but there wasn't enough information to determine if it did occur.

Elder abuse is reported in a similar manner.

This information is reported to county child protection or social services. The State Human Service Department collects this information in most states. The rate is the number of occurrences divided by the population. The population is the number of children under eighteen (for child

Finding information

abuse) and the number of people over age sixty-five for elder abuse. Multiply this number by 1,000 to get a rate per 1,000.

Record the rates of child abuse and elder abuse as number of occurrences and as a rate per 1,000 population on lines eighteen through thirty-seven of the Violent Events worksheet.

Suicide

Background   Suicide is one of the categories of violence discussed in this report. It is important to look at adults and teens separately: teen suicide is a significant problem in some communities and may not show up if the information is grouped with adults.

Finding information   Suicide information is found at the State Health Department.

Record the number and rate per 1,000 people on lines thirty-eight and thirty-nine of the Violent Events worksheet. For small communities it may make sense to use the numbers rather than the rate.

Other Sources of Information

The information we have suggested collecting is based on what we know is available due to various federal, state, county, or community reporting requirements. There may be additional information about specific types of violence in your community through community surveys and victim assistance agencies.

Some communities regularly conduct surveys and collect information about the level of victimization in their community. Sometimes these kinds of surveys are conducted in student populations. If your community conducts such surveys, you could add that information to Part 2 of the Community Report Card.

Victim assistance agencies, such as women's shelters, rape crisis centers, crisis telephone services, and so forth, often track violent incidents. Some of the information reported to such agencies may not appear in official police reports for various reasons: some victims are reluctant to go to the police, some are reluctant to press charges, and some police departments do not file such reports. You can use information from such agencies to compare to or augment the official numbers, or add as a separate line on Part 2 of the Community Report Card.

Part 3: Service Availability and Accessibility

Part 3 of the Community Report Card asks you to assess the availability and accessibility of services. We begin by asking you to find out if particular services are present, and then ask you to consider how easily each service can be accessed. *Presence* is objective and relatively easy to determine; either a service exists in your community, or it doesn't. Tracking down the service can be difficult, though, and we have suggested some possible sources of information in the following paragraph. *Access* is a more complicated assessment, as it combines a number of factors, such as how a potential client contacts the service, the relative cost of the service, and the hours during which it is available. Access is a subjective judgment, but we have included a series of questions for you to ask and a way to rate access based on those questions.

Presence

Information on the presence of a given service can be found through a number of sources:

- The white and yellow pages of the local phone book.

- Professional organizations for specific disciplines, many of which have directories.

- The local school district.

- Citizens' groups, such as Mothers Against Drunk Driving.

- Relevant social service, state, county, and municipal agencies.

You can use your contacts with one agency to help you find others.

For each service, record the presence or absence as a "yes" or "no" on the Service Availability and Accessibility worksheet.

Access

To assess the accessibility of the services, we've provided a series of questions you can ask about each service listed in Part 3 of the report card. We've proposed a scoring system to help you rate the accessibility of each service. Please note that the system is very subjective. Our only intent is to give you a starting point and way of comparing the relative accessibility of the services.

To figure an accessibility score, add up the total points for the service. A score of zero to seven indicates good accessibility; a score of eight to fifteen indicates fair accessibility; and a score of sixteen to twenty-two indicates poor accessibility. Not all the criteria above will apply to all services, some criteria may need adjustment, and conditions in your community may suggest other criteria to you. (For example, distances between services in some rural communities are automatically a barrier to access, but for comparative purposes, you may well want to adjust the criteria for the number of minutes it takes to reach a certain service.)

We suggest you enter the rating as good, fair, or poor on the Rating Service Accessibility worksheet on page 44. Add comments as needed.

Part 4: Monitoring the Information

We've created two worksheets to help you assemble, track, and analyze the information you have collected.

Part 4a: Community Comparisons

The first worksheet, Community Comparisons, allows you to study how your community compares with a community similar to yours. Comparing your community with a similar one may provide information about risk factors that are high or low or particular types of violence that requires attention. To use this worksheet, select a community or county to compare yours with. Such a community should be similar to yours in population, ethnic diversity, and family income; it's also helpful to pick one from the same region of your state. Record the information for both your community or county and the comparison community on the worksheet.

Part 4b: Comparisons over Time

The second worksheet, Comparisons over Time, allows you to track risk factors and violent events in your community over time. Over a period of several years you may notice changes in the numbers or rates. These changes may be due to the work the community is doing to change violent behavior. In some cases the number of violent events reported may increase if you are making people more aware of violence or if you have instituted a special program to respond to violence. Note that some information on the chart, such as low birth weight and suicide, may not be available for a city, township, or small community in a rural area. For these indicators, record the county-wide rates.

Community Report Card
Part 1: Community Risk Factors

Community: _____

Reporting period: _____ Year: _____

Community Composition	Number	Percent or Rate
1. Total population		NA
2. *Age:* Under 5		
3. 5-14		
4. 15-24		
5. 25-44		
6. 45-64		
7. 65 and older		
Diversity		
8. *Ethnicity:* Hispanic		
9. Non-Hispanic		
10. *Race:* Black		
11. White		
12. Asian		
13. Native American		
14. Other		
15. Religions (list)		
•		
•		
•		
•		
Economic Stress		
16. Percent single parent families		
17. Percent below poverty		
18. Percent unemployment		
19. Adults with high school diploma		
20. School attendance		
21. School dropout		
Health		
22. Low birth weight babies		
23. Mothers under age eighteen		
Alcohol and Other Drugs		
24. *Driving under the influence:* Teens		
25. Adults		
26. Narcotic crime reports		
27. Adolescent alcohol use		

41

Community Report Card

Part 2: Violent Events

Community: _____

Reporting period: _____ Year: _____

Violent Crimes	Number	Rate	Adult Offenders	Juvenile Offenders
Serious Crimes				
1. Murder and manslaughter (total)				
2. Domestic				
3. Nondomestic				
4. Rape				
5. Aggravated assault (total)				
6. Domestic				
7. Nondomestic				
8. Robbery				
Less Serious Crimes				
9. Minor assaults (total)				
10. Domestic				
11. Nondomestic				
12. Sexual offenses				
Other Information				
13. Weapon				
14. No weapon				
15. No weapon information				
16. Bias crimes				
17. Orders for protection				
Child Abuse				
18. Physical abuse (total)				
19. Substantiated				
20. Unsubstantiated				
21. Unable to substantiate				
22. Sexual abuse (total)				
23. Substantiated				
24. Unsubstantiated				
25. Unable to substantiate				
26. Emotional abuse (total)				
27. Substantiated				
28. Unsubstantiated				
29. Unable to substantiate				
30. Neglect (total)				
31. Substantiated				
32. Unsubstantiated				
33. Unable to substantiate				
Elder Abuse				
34. Elder abuse (total)				
35. Substantiated				
36. Unsubstantiated				
37. Unable to substantiate				
Suicides				
38. Adult				
39. Adolescent and child				

Community Report Card

Part 3: Service Availability and Accessibility

Community: _____

Reporting period: _____ Year: _____

Interventions	Yes	No	Accessibility	Comments
Hot line				
Hospital				
Police				
Mental health services				
County adult and child protection				
Ambulance				
Mediation				
Safe houses for children				
Group homes for teenagers				
Shelters or advocates for domestic abuse victims				
Rape and sexual assault counseling centers or advocates				
Respite care for caregivers for the elderly				
Foster care				
Services for victims of violent crime				
State and Federal civil rights offices				
Juvenile detention facilities				
Treatment				
Chemical dependency				
Gambling dependency				
Domestic abuse				
Other offender services				
Prevention and Public Education				
Prenatal and child health services				
Quality recreational activities for young people				
Workplace programs on assault, substance abuse, suicide, harassment, and diversity				
Firearm safety programs for adults and children				
Parenting classes				
Caregiver education and support				
School programs				
Alcohol/drug prevention				
Violence prevention/conflict resolution				
Suicide prevention				
Media coverage that educates				

Community Report Card
Rating Service Accessibility

To assess the accessibility of services, ask the following questions about each service listed in Part 3 of the report card. We've proposed a scoring system to help you rate the accessibility of each service. Please note that the system is very subjective. Our only intent is to give you a starting point and way of comparing the relative accessibility of the services.

Accessibility Score	
0-7 points	= good
8-15 points	= fair
16-22 points	= poor

Criteria   **Score**

1. Does access require driving a car?
   No = 0   Yes = 2   _____

2. If a car is required, how many minutes does it take to reach the service?
   < 20 minutes = 0   20-40 minutes = 1   > 40 minutes = 2   _____

3. Does access require a phone?
   No = 0   Yes = 2   _____

4. If a phone is required, is the call long distance?
   No = 0   Yes = 2   _____

5. If the service involves the provider coming to the victim,
   does the average response time match the victim's needs?
   Yes = 0   No = 2   _____

6. Is medical insurance required to receive services?
   No = 0   Yes = 2   _____

7. Is the cost of services affordable to the victim?
   Yes = 0   No = 2   _____

8. Are referrals regularly offered—does the initial contact (police, emergency room,
   health professional, counselor) provide referrals to other appropriate services
   (especially between police, medical, victim services, county protection)?
   Yes = 0   No = 2   _____

9. Are professionals adequately trained to respond to violence?
   Yes = 0   No = 2   _____

10. Is the service available during hours when the client can conveniently use it
    (for example, after work and on weekends)?
    Yes = 0   No = 2   _____

11. Do clients wait or get turned away from services?
    No = 0   Yes = 2   _____

Total Score   _____

Community Report Card

Part 4a: Community Comparisons

Community: _____ Year: _____

Risk Factors	Your Community	Your County	Comparison Community	Comparison County	State
Population					
Percent below poverty					
Percent white					
Percent single parents					
Percent of mothers under age eighteen					
Percent low birth weight					
Percent unemployment					
Percent of adults with a high school diploma					
Suicide rate					
Driving under the influence rate					
Narcotics crimes rate					
Violent Events					
Serious crimes					
Murder rate					
Rape rate					
Aggravated assault rate—domestic					
Aggravated assault rate—nondomestic					
Robbery rate					
Less serious crimes					
Bias crimes					
Orders of protection					
Minor assault rate—domestic					
Minor assault rate—nondomestic					
Sexual offenses rate					
Child abuse rate (all reports)					
Physical abuse rate					
Sexual abuse rate					
Emotional abuse rate					
Neglect rate					
Elder abuse rate (all reports)					
Suicide Rate					

NOTE: All crimes, abuse, and risk factors are calculated as rates per 1,000 when possible.

Community Report Card
Part 4b: Comparisons over Time

Community: _____

Risk Factors	Year: Community	County	Year: Community	County	Year: Community	County
Population						
Percent below poverty						
Percent white						
Percent single parents						
Percent of mothers under age eighteen						
Percent low birth weight						
Percent unemployment						
Percent of adults with a high school diploma						
Suicide rate						
Driving under the influence rate						
Narcotics crimes rate						
Violent Events						
Serious crimes						
Murder rate						
Rape rate						
Aggravated assault rate—domestic						
Aggravated assault rate—nondomestic						
Robbery rate						
Less serious crimes						
Bias crimes						
Orders of protection						
Minor assault rate—domestic						
Minor assault rate—nondomestic						
Sexual offenses rate						
Child abuse rate (all reports)						
Physical abuse rate						
Sexual abuse rate						
Emotional abuse rate						
Neglect rate						
Elder abuse rate (all reports)						
Suicide Rate						

NOTE: All crimes, abuse, and risk factors are calculated as rates per 1,000 when possible.

46

▌Literature Review Matrix

A. Assaultive Violence

Fatal and nonfatal interpersonal violence where physical force or other means is used by one person with the intent of causing harm, injury or death to another (Rosenberg and Fenley, 1991).

Types of Efforts	Effectiveness	Rural Specific
Prevention		
1. Schoolwide interventions to reduce bullying and aggressive behavior in children. Emphasis is on positive behavior, involvement of teachers and parents, setting firm limits on unacceptable behavior, and the use of nonhostile, noncorporal sanctions for rule violations.	This approach has increased student satisfaction with school and has reduced bullying behavior as well as thefts, vandalism, and truancy (Olweus, 91; Hawkins, et al., 91; Patterson in Farrington, et al., 86).	Has been shown to be effective in rural and urban communities (Olweus, 91).
2. Teaching conflict resolution and problem-solving skills.	Has shown success in reducing violence in elementary and high school age students (Eron, 86; Reiss and Roth, 93; Larson, 92).	Program in rural community was successful in increasing social support among students. Important to have a person from the community as coordinator (Mooney, 86).
3. Training and educating about different cultures (diversity training).	The most successful approaches have been to put people from different ethnic and racial groups into small teams to work together to accomplish a task (Goleman, 91).	No study.
4. Reduce delinquent behavior.	Successful programs to reduce delinquent behavior in teens are community-based, provide case management, are highly intensive, focus on the family, and provide referral to a wide variety of services (Howitt and Moore, 93; Kumpfer, 93; Roundtree, et al., 93; Binder, in Farrington, et al., 86).	No study.

A. Assaultive Violence (continued)

Types of Efforts	Effectiveness	Rural Specific
5. Education about television violence.	Interventions that work on changing children's attitudes about television violence have been most successful in changing imitative behavior (Eron, 86).	No study.
6. Increase the availability of prenatal and postnatal health care.	No studies have shown effectiveness in reducing violence, yet there is a link between violence and children who are low birth weight or premature; such children are more at risk for language and speech disorders, balance and coordination problems, and perceptual and spatial problems, which have been linked to the development of crime and violence (Reiss and Roth, 93).	No study.
7. Reduce school failure.	School failure is an important predictor of those people who later commit violent acts (Reiss and Roth, 93). The Perry Preschool Study showed that children who received Head Start-like services were less likely to be arrested as teens than those who didn't participate in the program (Berreuta-Clement, et al., in Farrington, et al., 86).	Head Start for migrant families successfully used bilingual paraprofessionals to teach migrant children (Tan, et. al., 91).
8. Reduce the consumption of drugs and alcohol.	Abuse and use of drugs and alcohol strongly associated with violent acts (Reiss and Roth, 93; Rosenberg, 91). Successful school-based programs that affect young people's drug use are those that teach social competency skills. School-based programs that have shown a lasting effect on alcohol and drug use offer booster sessions in later grades or have broadened the program to involve parents, media, and the community in promoting norms against drug use (Hawkins, et al., 92). Alcohol drinking and violence are linked through pharmacological effects on behavior, through expectations that heavy drinking and violence go together in certain settings, and through patterns of binge drinking and fighting that sometimes develop in adolescence. The most promising strategies for reducing alcohol-related violence are to reduce underage drinking through substance abuse preventive education, taxes, law enforcement, and peer pressure (Roth, 94).	No study.
9. Increase the prosecution of all types of assaultive violence.	Believed to be a deterrent (Reiss and Roth, 93).	No study.

A. Assaultive Violence (continued)

Types of Efforts	Effectiveness	Rural Specific
10. Reduce access to firearms or make it more difficult to acquire a firearm.	Has been shown to be effective in reducing homicides and suicides in an urban environment (Reiss and Roth, 93). Gun restriction generally has no effect upon violence rates, with the following exceptions: • additional penalties for robberies with guns may reduce robbery rate; • requiring permits to buy guns may reduce suicide rate; • licensing may reduce aggravated assault, robbery, and suicide rates; • banning gun possession by mentally ill people may reduce suicides (Kleck and Patterson, 93).	No study.
11. Conflict resolution training in schools and community.	See G-6.	No study.
12. Neighborhood mediation centers.	Mediation centers have been shown to be helpful and successful in resolving disputes peacefully (Shonholtz, 87).	No study.
13. Reduce poverty.	Poverty is a factor for all kinds of assaultive violence (Reiss and Roth, 93; Rosenberg and Mercy, 91).	No study.
14. Victim assistance services.	See C-11.	No study.
15. Victim-offender mediation.	Victims of nonviolent crimes were less fearful of re-victimization after mediation (Umbreit, 93). Case studies show victims of violent crimes find benefits (Umbreit, 89).	Umbreit study includes rural communities.
16. Available trauma and health treatment.	Physical and psychological treatment helpful and necessary for victims (Rosenberg and Mercy, 91).	No study.
Services to Offenders (Adults and Juveniles)		
17. Social skills training—interventions that teach aggressive juveniles to have better self-control, understand their feelings, listen more carefully, and improve their problem-solving skills.	Has shown success with children over a period of time (Reiss and Roth, 93).	No study.

A. Assaultive Violence (continued)

Types of Efforts	Effectiveness	Rural Specific
18. Parent effectiveness training and family strengthening.	Has been shown to be successful in reducing aggression in children, particularly when combined with teacher effectiveness training (Reiss and Roth, 93; Kumpfer, 93).	No study.
19. Incarceration—adult.	Successful only when combined with rehabilitative services (Andrews, et al., 90).	No study.
Incarceration—juvenile.	Successful and humane maximum security units for juveniles have the following components: • small units • individualized treatment • highly trained staff • small staff to youth ratio • strong emphasis on aftercare (Center for the Study of Youth Policy, 89; Office of Juvenile Justice and Delinquency Prevention, 93).	
20. Shock incarceration.	No more effective than traditional prison at reducing recidivism. Anecdotal evidence suggests that it helps some offenders (Mackenzie, 90; Mackenzie, et al., 93).	No study.
21. Restitution—juvenile.	In four different communities, juveniles were randomly assigned to either restitution or traditional sanctions. The experimental findings showed restitution has a small but important effect upon reducing recidivism (Schneider, 86).	No study.
22. Juvenile offender treatment programs.	Home-based programs for serious and violent offenders have similar recidivism rates as highly secure programs. Successful programs offer intensive supervision, small client case loads, and frequent client-worker contact (Center for the Study of Youth Policy, 89). Community approaches that provide a system of "graduated sanctions" had a substantial impact on post program arrests, court appearances, and violent offenses among chronic offenders (Office of Juvenile Justice and Delinquency Prevention, 93). Both group and family therapy seem to be effective modes of treatment for adolescent offenders (Roberts and Camasso, 91). Intensive treatment program rates of recidivism of 33 to 46 percent. Yet, considering these youth	No study.

A. Assaultive Violence (continued)

Types of Efforts	Effectiveness	Rural Specific
	were considered to be at 100 percent risk of reoffending, the intensive program was seen to be quite effective (Hagen and King, 92).	
	Juvenile treatment program found better success rates for youth who were older and stayed longer (Giacobbe, 88).	
	Effective programs included a cognitive treatment approach or modeling (Sarason and Ganzer in Farrington, et al., 86; Izzo and Ross, 90).	
23. Swift prosecution.	Immediate consequences to the offender has been shown to reduce repeat crimes (Reiss and Roth, 93; Greenwood, 82).	No study.
24. Reentry programs provide offenders who have been incarcerated with counseling, education, employment counseling, housing, and social support upon reentry into the community.	Evidence of effectiveness (Bartollas, 85). Assistance given to offenders reentering the community led to decreased recidivism (Berntsen and Christianson, Shaw, Rossi, et al., in Farrington, 86).	No study.
25. Alcohol and other drug abuse treatment programs.	Adolescent substance abusers who received treatment had less recidivism than those who do not receive treatment (Roberts and Camasso, 91). Therapeutic communities for drug offenders show some success but have a high dropout rate (Bartollas, 85).	No study.
26. Victim-offender mediation.	Some studies have shown that juvenile offenders in victim-offender mediation programs committed considerably fewer crimes than matched samples of similar offenders not in mediation (Umbreit, 93).	No study.
27. Alternatives to incarceration.	Controlled study of effective community-based alternatives to incarceration for young adult offenders (Owens, 84; Owen and Mattessich, 88). Lower levels of recidivism for community-based program graduates than those who were incarcerated. Probation Day Centers found to be as effective as incarceration on recidivism rates (Vass, 90).	No study. ■

B₁. Child Abuse

The physical or mental injury, sexual abuse, negligent treatment, or maltreatment of a child under the age of eighteen by a person who is responsible for the child's welfare under circumstances which would indicate that the child's health or welfare is harmed or threatened thereby (The Federal Child Abuse Prevention and Treatment Act of 1974, PL 93-237).

Types of Efforts	Effectiveness	Rural Specific
Prevention		
1. Prenatal and postnatal health care for women.	Helps mothers bond with children, reduces the likelihood of having a premature or disabled child at high risk for abuse (Reiss and Roth, 93).	Case management, home visits, and use of midwives have been effective in rural communities (Wheeler, et al., 92).
2. Parent hot lines to reduce stress.	Little evidence that these are effective in preventing maltreatment (Mueller and Higgins, 88).	No study.
3. Parenting education and support.	Social learning model of parent education shown to be effective. Needs to be integrated with other services that address social isolation, unemployment, and poverty (Gaudin, Jr., 85). No studies on effectiveness of parent education in schools. Home visiting and programs in centers found improved mother-infant bonding, ability to care for child, and ability to employ nonphysical methods of discipline (Daro, 88; Morgan, et al., 90; Mueller and Higgins, 88).	Classes should be located geographically close to parents and child care should be provided. Sensitivity to reading and cognitive levels of parents appear in most successful programs (Grayson and McNulty, 82). Newsletters about parenting in the first year have been shown to be helpful (Sjolln and Riley, 93). Parenting programs for women in battered women's shelters helpful (Hughes, 86). Groups held in homes of participants successful (Kline, et al., 90).
4. School-based education programs.	Classroom education helpful when combined with community networking, parent training, and change in school atmosphere (Derezotes and Barth, 93).	Use of volunteers in providing school-based educational programs have been successful in rural areas (Ray and Murty, 90).

B₁. Child Abuse (continued)

Types of Efforts	Effectiveness	Rural Specific
5. Comprehensive prevention programs for at-risk families.	This approach, though costly, has been effective with some families including poor and young mothers, in both urban and rural communities. It includes in-home education and supportive services in conjunction with support group attendance. Effective programs incorporate the following goals: • Increasing parent's knowledge of child development and role of parent. • Enhancing parent's skills in coping with stress of parenting. • Enhancing child bonding and communication. • Increasing parent's knowledge about home and child management. • Reducing the burden of child care. • Increasing access to social and health services for all family members (Daro, 88; Kowal, et al., 89; Hardy and Strueett, 89; Wesch and Lutzker, 91; Gaudin Jr., 93). Home Builders Program showed 86 percent of children avoided placement. Less successful with neglectful parents or multiple cases of maltreatment (Bath, and Haapala, 93).	See Effectiveness category.
6. The use of trained volunteers and paraprofessional intervention workers. Training nonprofessional people in the community to provide support and education to families at risk of abusing their children.	This approach has been effective. Better for less chronically abusive parents (Barth, 91).	Has been shown to be very effective in rural communities (Connors, 83; Shybut, 82; Grayson and McNulty, 82; Sefcik and Ormsby, 78; Ganong and Coleman, 83). Use of "natural helpers" successful in migrant community (Gerdean, 91).
7. Public awareness campaigns.	Has been shown to increase knowledge (Mueller and Higgins, 88).	No study.
8. Establish and implement model protocols for the early identification and referral of abuse victims in health settings.	Research and technological advances have increased physician's ability to detect abuse (National Research Council, 93). Reports filed by physicians function as strong cues to child protection to investigate and validate abuse (Warner and Hansen, 94).	No study.

B₁. Child Abuse (continued)

Types of Efforts	Effectiveness	Rural Specific
9. Counseling (individual, family, or group therapy)	Has been shown to be helpful for child abuse victims. For most successful intervention parents must accept treatment. Teaching social skills to adolescents and children who have been abused helps them relate to peer groups, which reduces social isolation (Fantuzzo and Holland, 92; Feldman, et al., in Farrington, et al., 86). No studies have been done to determine the most effective treatment approaches for children who have been abused or children who have witnessed family violence. Group therapy for adult incest survivors has helped to relieve symptoms (Reith, 90). No systematic evaluation has been done to determine most effective treatments (Daro, 88).	No study.
10. Criminal justice reforms, limiting the number of interviews, expediting cases.	Videotaping reduces the trauma of multiple interviews (Myers, John, 93). Videotaping, joint interviews, and coordinating court proceedings have streamlined the process and limited the number of interviews. Swift prosecution is less damaging to children (Whitcomb, 92).	No study.
11. Cooperation among agencies such as criminal justice, child protection, health care, and mental health agencies.	Favorable outcomes occur for children when coordinated services are available (Rosenberg and Fenley, 91).	Training and coordination necessary for providing service in rural areas (Ray and Murty, 90). Coordination increased early identification of families (Schechter, 81).
12. Therapeutic day care that includes monitoring of nutrition and health.	Substantial gains have been reported for children in these programs (Daro, 88).	No study.
13. Guardian ad litem—individual appointed by the court to represent child's best interest.	Lay advocates may be more effective than attorneys in representing the best interests of children by providing counseling, protecting against system-induced trauma, coordinating actions of multiple agencies, and advocating the child's legal rights (Whitcomb, 92).	No study.
14. Children's centers—central location dedicated to streamlining and simplifying the investigation process.	Useful in acquiring children's testimony in a less threatening way. Streamlines and simplifies investigation process (Whitcomb, 92).	No study.

B₁. Child Abuse (continued)

Types of Efforts	Effectiveness	Rural Specific
15. Foster care and shelters.	Children's behavioral and developmental problems improve (Daro, 88).	Shelters offer protection and an opportunity to develop a relationship with a trusted adult for teens in rural communities (Dimock, 80).
Services for Offenders 16. Therapy for abusing parents.	Individual therapy is less successful than group or family therapy. Family therapy is the treatment of choice for sexual abuse and incest. Behavioral techniques without physical force taught so parents can control child's behavior. Therapy based on social learning behavior theory has shown some success. Programs to halt severe physical neglect and psychological maltreatment have been ineffective. Relationship-building between parent and child shows some success (Daro, 88; Howing, et al., 89).	No study.
17. Chemical dependency treatment.	No studies on effectiveness in reducing child abuse.	No study. ∎

B_2. Child Sexual Abuse

Sexual contact with a child that occurs as a result of force in a relationship where it is exploitative because of an age difference or caretaking responsibility (Rosenberg and Fenley, 1991).

Types of Efforts	Effectiveness	Rural Specific
Prevention		
1. Sexual abuse prevention programs for children.	Have been shown to increase children's knowledge of what sexual abuse is and what to do if it happens (Daro, 88).	No study.
Such programs are primarily educational; they teach children what sexual abuse is, what to do if it happens, and how to get help.		
Interventions		
2. Education for professionals (reporting, identification, referral).	Physicians trained in the examination of sexually abused children are able to gauge the need for long term follow-up and support for children (Levitt, et al., 94).	No study.
Services for Victims		
3. Counseling (individual, family, or group therapy).	Has been shown to be helpful for child sex abuse victims. Parents must accept their children's treatment for most successful intervention. Group treatment has been shown to reduce problem behaviors (Hiebert-Murphy, et al., 92; Daro, 88).	No study.
4. Cooperation among agencies such as criminal justice, child protection, health care, and mental health agencies.	See Child Abuse section.	Training and coordination necessary for providing services in rural areas (Ray and Murty, 90). Coordination increased early identification of families (Schechter, 81).
Services for Offenders		
5. Juvenile sexual abuse offender treatment programs.	Peer group treatment combined with a system of incentives found effective (Smets, 87). See Rape and Sexual Assault Treatment for Offenders.	Treatment program in rural Wisconsin found peer group therapy combined with individual and family therapy and system of incentives had low incidence of recidivism, and clients rated the program highly (Smets, 87).

B$_2$. Child Sexual Abuse (continued)

Types of Efforts	Effectiveness	Rural Specific
6. Criminal sanctions.	Useful in getting participation from offenders and in keeping them away from victims (Rosenberg and Mercy, 91).	No study.
7. Adult sexual abuse offender treatment programs.	Peer group treatment combined with group therapy and education. Behavioral treatment has shown some success. No systematic evaluation has been done to determine what combination of therapies works best. Hormonal, group, family, and behavioral therapies have been successful with some offenders (Becker and Hunter, 92). A cost-benefit analysis indicates the cost of *not* treating child molesters to be $67,988.05 more than treating them (Prentky and Burgess, 92).	No study. ∎

C. Rape and Sexual Assault

Nonconsensual oral, anal, or vaginal penetration obtained through the use of force or threat of force (Rosenberg and Fenley, 1991).

Types of Efforts	Effectiveness	Rural Specific
Prevention		
1. Education about date rape and sexual assault in schools.	Can change attitudes, knowledge, and behavioral intentions (Jaffe, et al., 92). Prevention programs that emphasize role-playing and practice skills have been found to be more effective in changing behavior than strictly informational programs.	No study.
2. Reduction in pornography.	There is believed to be a relationship between pornography and rape. However, in Kimmel's (93) review of research studies in this area no direct associations were found. In one study reviewed by Kimmel, the amount of exposure to sexually explicit materials during adolescence were actually lower for deviants and sex offenders than their control groups. Another study reviewed by Kimmel looked at levels of aggression after viewing sexually explicit material compared to other types of material. They found that men responded more aggressively to violent films than sexually explicit ones.	No study.
3. Risk awareness and self-defense programs.	No study.	No study.
Interventions		
4. Establish and implement model protocols for the early identification and referral of rape and sexual assault victims in health settings.	Programs that seem to be most effective in serving the needs of rape victims are those that are integrated with medical, mental health, and legal professionals (Koss and Harvey, 87).	No study.
5. Cooperation among agencies such as criminal justice, health care, and mental health agencies.	Improved treatment of rape victims may function as a method of crime prevention (Rosenberg and Fenley, 91, p. 98).	Training and coordination necessary for providing services in rural areas (Ray and Murty, 90).

C. Rape and Sexual Assault (continued)

Types of Efforts	Effectiveness	Rural Specific
6. Crisis telephone services.	Believed helpful; little evaluative research (Bleach and Claiborn,74; Gingerich, et al., 88).	Effective in reducing stress and linking people to services in rural areas (Adams and Benjamin, 88). Access to crisis line services are particularly important in rural areas (Edleson and Frank, 91).
7. Treatment of adolescent sex offenders.	Considering the number of adult sex offenders that commit their first offense in their early teens, treating adolescent sex offenders seems to be an effective prevention strategy (Benoit and Kennedy, 92; Bremer, 92; California Criminal Justice Planning Office, 91; Smets, 87).	No study.
Services for Victims		
8. Counseling (individual, family, or group).	Effective in reducing depression and increasing social adjustment (Alexander, et al., 91; Patten, et al., 89). Some specific treatment modalities have been found to show better results with treating trauma related to rape (Foa, et al., 93).	Peer support groups for mental health problems were found to be helpful in rural communities. Activities and outreach are conducted outside of the mental health offices, in places such as community organizations, churches, schools and businesses to help reach an often resistant population (Adams and Benjamin, 88).
9. Advocacy—the use of trained staff to assist victims of rape or domestic assault to hospitals and with the criminal justice system.	Believed to help but no studies of effectiveness (Von, et al., 91).	No study.
10. Victim-offender mediation.	Mediation with some rape victims is believed to be beneficial in helping the victim gain a sense of closure and healing (Sauter, 93).	No study.

C. Rape and Sexual Assault (continued)

Types of Efforts	Effectiveness	Rural Specific
Services for Offenders		
11. Swift prosecution.	Immediate consequences to the offender's crime believed to reduce repeat crimes (Reiss and Roth, 93; Greenwood, 82). In some states, changes in the rape laws to four different degrees of sexual assault have resulted in a higher conviction rate (Caringella-MacDonald, 84).	No study.
12. Drug therapy (chemical castration).	MPA (Medrox Progesterone Acetate) treatment has been found to be effective with paraphiliacs: "those persons compelled to commit sex crimes in order to realize a specific and particularized sexual fantasy" (Fitzgerald, 90).	No study.
13. Treatment or counseling.	Social skills training as part of treatment is believed to be beneficial (Graves, et al., 92). Techniques found to have positive outcomes for adult sex offenders used a multimodal approach and coordinated treatment with other agencies such as child protection, prisons, and parole officers (Schwartz, 92). Residential treatment programs with services for adolescent sex offenders had similar outcomes as specialized sex treatment programs (Brannon and Troyer, 91). Recidivism rates vary with each program. One program found to be effective for juveniles had a recidivism rate of 6 percent after long-term follow-up of all released residents (Bremer, 92; Becker and Kaplan, 92). Another program had a recidivism rate of 2.5 percent for sexual reoffenses with an average follow-up of fifteen months (California Criminal Justice Planning Office, 91). Most effective treatment of violent sex offenders is a combination of incarceration, psychotherapy, and hormonal therapy (Sadoff, 86). Not all the studies agree. For example, one study found no conclusive evidence that sex offenders programs reduce recidivism (Quinsey, et al., 93).	Group treatment program working in conjunction with individual and family therapy in rural midwestern town (Smets, 87). ■

D. Domestic Abuse

The use of physical force in intimate relationships among adults (Rosenberg and Fenley, 1991).

Types of Efforts	Effectiveness	Rural Specific
Prevention		
1. Public awareness and education about spouse abuse.	No study.	No study.
2. School-based education programs to increase awareness of physical abuse.	Evaluation of high school programs to prevent violence in intimate relationships found an increase in positive attitudes. However, gender differences were found with females showing more positive attitudes than males (Jaffe, et al., 92). Another study also showed an increase in positive attitudes (Rosenbluth, 92).	This study found domestic abuse in rural areas to be similar to that of urban areas, but found that rural areas lack services, trained professionals, and community information. The study also recommended that prevention programs work through public school curriculum and adolescent health programs (Rosen, 81).
3. Cooperation among agencies such as criminal justice, child protection, health care, and mental health agencies.	Coordinated efforts by authorities resulting in arrest of abuser followed by court mandated treatment are more likely to end violence (Syers and Edleson, 92 as cited in Edleson and Tolman, 92).	Training and coordination necessary for providing services in rural areas (Ray and Murty, 90). Coordination increased early identification of families (Schechter, 81). Found to be effective mode of getting information and services to those in crisis, given the limited resources available in rural areas (Silver and Goldstein, 92; Hamlin II, 91).
Services for Victims		
4. Crisis telephone services.	Gingerich, et al., (88) found that helplines were perceived to be helpful by callers.	Access to crisis telephone services is particularly important in rural areas (Edleson and Frank, 91).

D. Domestic Abuse (continued)

Types of Efforts	Effectiveness	Rural Specific
5. Citizen intervention and neighborhood conflict resolution programs.	No effectiveness studies. Believed to be a good method of prevention because such programs resolve conflicts before they escalate (Shonholtz, 87).	No study.
6. Police and citizen intervention teams.	Police training on issues surrounding domestic abuse was found to increase referrals to outside agencies (Buzawa and Buzawa, 90) The victim's preference in the outcome of police intervention is important. A Detroit study found that fewer women were willing to call the police because of their mandatory arrest policy, in which the women had less control of the outcome (Buzawa and Buzawa, 90).	"Increased residential stability and religious involvement, as preventive measures, are likely to be more effective in rural areas" (Byrne, 77).
7. Establish and implement model health care protocols for the early identification and referral of abuse victims.	The use of a team approach that joins all agencies and services together is believed to help reduce fragmentation of services and promote consistent and standardized interventions for victims (Hamlin II, 91).	No study.
8. Counseling (individual, family, group).	Effective in reducing depression and increasing social adjustment (Alexander, et al., 91). Groups for children in domestic abuse shelters shown to be helpful (Hughes, 86). Increases in self-esteem and reduction of violence for program participants (Tutty et al., 93).	Support groups for victims and offenders of domestic abuse is an effective strategy in rural areas. Particularly, a combination of support groups, therapy, and awareness education is believed to work well in rural areas (Andrews, 90).
9. Safe houses, shelters, and safe wards in local health care facilities.	Shown to be effective in reducing violence. Domestic violence decreased 6.6 percent from 1974 to 1985, when shelters were established (Straus and Gelles, 90).	Shelters and safe houses have been located in rural areas (Edleson and Frank, 1991).
10. Advocacy—the use of trained staff to assist victims of rape or domestic assault to hospitals and with criminal justice system.	Believed to be effective (Williams-White in Dickstein and Nadelson, 89; Edleson, 93).	No study.

D. Domestic Abuse (continued)

Types of Efforts	Effectiveness	Rural Specific
11. Victim assistance services—may include services such as in-house counseling, shelter, phone counseling, food, legal information, transportation, clothing, and child care.	No study.	Rural programs were found to offer a wider range of services than urban programs. Transportation and physical proximity are important factors influencing use of programs in rural areas (Bogal-Allbrittenand Rogers Daughaday, 90.)
12. Orders for protection and restraining orders.	Found to be effective in reducing violence, but only with couples where the injuries in the past were not severe. No reduction for the most violent abusers (Grau, et al., 84).	No study.
Services for Offenders		
13. Swift prosecution.	Immediate consequences to the offenders believed to reduce repeat offenses (Reiss and Roth, 93; Greenwood, 82).	No study.
14. Arrest and incarceration.	One study found the length of incarceration did not make a difference in recidivism rates. Arrest with mandated treatment for spouse abusers has been shown to reduce recidivism for employed men (Clark, 93). Effectiveness of arrest in reducing recidivism varies greatly; in some cases it has positive effects, while in others it has negative effects (Rosenberg and Fenley, 91; Sherman, 92 as cited in Schmidt and Sherman, 93; Hilton, 94).	No study.
15. Alcohol and drug abuse treatment programs.	Concurrent treatment of substance abuse seems to be important for successful therapy (Geffner and Pagelow, 90; Shepard, 92).	No study.

D. Domestic Abuse (continued)

Types of Efforts	Effectiveness	Rural Specific
16. Spouse abuse treatment programs use a wide variety of techniques including behavioral modification, individual therapy, education, peer support, and contact with victims (but not the perpetrators' own victims).	Studies comparing various treatment strategies have not been done (Rosenbaum and Maiuro, 90). Some elements of some programs have been shown to be effective while other elements are not. A study of fifteen different outcome studies on batterers who went through domestic abuse treatment had a range of 46 to 87 percent success rate. What was considered a "success" varied; most studies meant that the physical violence stopped (Edleson and Tolman, 92). Couple's therapy has been shown to be detrimental to victims of abuse and is not effective in curbing abuse (Gondolf, 92). Court mandated treatment, if completed, was found to reduce violence (Syers and Edleson, 92; Gondolf, 92; Hamlin II, 91; Straus and Gelles, 90). Learning about how the abusive behavior has affected other victims of spouse abuse has made an impact upon offenders, with a 40 percent recidivism rate five years after offenders treatment program (Shepard, 92).	No study.
17. Self-help groups.	Believed helpful when combined with other interventions. These are programs such as modified twelve-step groups (Geffner and Pagelow, 90).	No study.
18. Couple therapy and couple group treatment.	Couple therapy and couple group therapy have mixed results of effectiveness. Recidivism varies from 100 percent in one study to 15 percent in another at a six month follow-up (Edleson, 90). Although there have been no experimental evaluations done of group treatment, many studies have found lower recidivism rates for completers of programs as compared with the recidivism rates of those who dropped out of treatment (Edleson, 90; Edleson and Tolman, 92).	No study. ■

E. Elder Abuse

An act of commission or omission that jeopardizes the well-being or safety of an elderly individual. The maltreatment of the elder may occur in the home and may include the following dimensions: physical abuse, emotional abuse, neglect or deprivation, material exploitation, sexual exploitation, and physical or verbal assault (Lucas, 1991).

Types of Efforts	Effectiveness	Rural Specific
Prevention		
1. Reduce social isolation in families through home visiting programs and development of an active social support network.	No study.	No study.
2. Public awareness of and education about the aging process.	A curriculum designed to explain the aging process and improve the communication and problem-solving skills of families with older adults was positively received (Gold and Gwyther, 89).	No study.
Interventions		
3. Establish and implement model health care protocols for the early identification and referral of abuse victims.	Elder abuse assessment team raises health care staff awareness and willingness to refer suspected cases (Carr, 86).	No study.
4. Cooperation among agencies such as criminal justice, adult protection, health care, mental health, and legal services.	Found to be effective and critical to getting information and services to those in crisis (Pillemer and Frankel, 91; Wolf and Pillemer, 89).	Training and coordination necessary for providing services in rural areas (Ray and Murty, 90). Coordination increased early identification of families (Schechter, 81).
5. Crisis telephone services.	Successful in making referrals and mobilizing police assistance (Wolf and Pillemer, 89).	No study.
Services for Victims		
6. Counseling (individual, family, group).	Effective in reducing depression and increasing social adjustment (Alexander, et al., 91). Family therapy helpful in some cases (Schlesinger, 88). Support groups helpful (Wolf and Pillemer, 89).	No study.
7. Community supports to reduce social isolation, and offer home visits, day care, respite care, and so forth.	Helpful in reducing strain between victim and abuser (Schlesinger, 88; Pillemer and Frankel, 91).	No study.

E. Elder Abuse (continued)

Types of Efforts	Effectiveness	Rural Specific
8. Case management.	Important in coordinating psychological, medical, legal, and environmental interventions (Pillemer and Frankel, 91).	No study.
9. Emergency shelters.	Safe houses for adults in Finland successful, foster homes in Vermont effective (Wolf and Pillemer, 89).	No study.
Services for Offenders		
10. Comprehensive services for the perpetrator.	Broad range of services (education, counseling, homemaker, self-sufficiency, employment, and support to reduce dependency of abuser on victim) (Schlesinger, 88).	No study. ■

F. Suicide

The act of taking one's life voluntarily and intentionally.

Types of Efforts	Effectiveness	Rural Specific
Prevention		
1. Prevention programs in the schools—two main approaches exist: some target all youth and some target only high risk youth.	Youth who are at high risk may react negatively (Center for Disease Control and Prevention, 92). School-based suicide prevention programs are effective in changing attitudes commonly believed to influence suicide completion (Ciffone, 93).	No study.
2. Access to counseling and psychological services.	Roy and Glaister (84) found that psychiatric patients who committed suicide had less frequent appointments than noncompleters (cited in Berman and Jobes, 91).	On-site services and training of elders on reservations is needed due to the physical distance from other available services and lack of telephones by many reservation tenants (Long, 86).
3. Limit access to common means of suicide such as firearms, prescription drugs, and high places.	Holinger (84) estimated that restricting access to firearms would reduce youth suicide by approximately 20 percent (cited in Berman and Jobes, 91).	No study.
4. Walk-in centers for counseling and referral.	The effectiveness of crisis centers at preventing suicides within specific communities has varied. Some communities show results that indicate possible effectiveness while others do not (Diekstra, 92).	No study.
5. School-based education programs to increase awareness of sexual abuse, physical abuse, date rape, and suicide.	Victims of child sexual abuse, physical abuse, and rape are at much higher risk of attempting suicide (Holub, et al., 1992). Programs focused on awareness of these issues are believed to be effective in helping reduce isolation and suicide.	No study.
6. Crisis telephone services.	Believed helpful; number of studies has been small and results have been mixed (Bleach and Claiborn, 74, Center for Disease Control and Prevention, 92). Callers of crisis telephone lines perceived services to be helpful (Gingerich, et al., 88). Those who use crisis centers and hot lines are at much higher risk of suicide than general population (Berman and Jobes, 91).	No study.

F. Suicide (continued)

Types of Efforts	Effectiveness	Rural Specific
7. Community intervention team.	Believed to be effective (Silver and Goldstein, 92).	Members of various agencies work together to provide services and training for crisis situations on a county level (Silver and Goldstein, 92).
8. Substance abuse treatment.	Treatment of underlying risk factors, such as alcoholism, is believed to help reduce suicidal tendencies (Rosenberg and Fenley, 91; Shaffer, 93).	No study.
9. Training for health care workers to recognize, treat, and refer patients.	Believed to help prevent suicide (Rosenberg and Fenley, 91).	No study.
Services for Victims (Attemptors, their families, and friends)		
10. Counseling (individual, family, group).	Effective in reducing depression and increasing social adjustment (Alexander, et al., 1991). Therapy for adult incest survivors has helped to relieve suicidal symptoms. No systematic evaluation has been done to determine best treatments.	Peer support groups found to be helpful in rural communities for mental health problems. Having activities and outreach outside the mental health offices is believed to be helpful in reaching resistant populations (Adams, et al., 88). For farmers under economic stress, family therapy with an emphasis on changing gender roles is believed to be effective in reducing stress and preventing suicide (Ragland and Berman, 90-91). ■

G. Bias Crimes (Crimes Motivated by Racism, Sexism, or Bigotry)

Discrimination based on gender or race. Intolerance of another's religion, culture, politics, sexual preference, or opinion.

Types of Efforts	Effectiveness	Rural Specific
Prevention		
1. Diversity training.	Successful approaches have combined members of different groups together into teams to accomplish a task (Goleman, 91).	No study.
2. Cooperative learning—systematic teaching approach to increase interpersonal communication skills.	Believed to help students gain skills in understanding perspectives other than their own (Deutsch, 93).	No study.
3. Religious initiatives against racism (cooperation among different religious organizations and within individual denominations).	No studies, yet there are a wide variety of programs.	No study.
4. Broad-based community efforts aimed at violence prevention and the promotion of peaceful living.	No studies, yet there are a wide variety of programs.	No study.
Interventions		
5. Mediation programs.	There are both school and community-based programs. Some research indicates a reduction in violence due to mediation (Deutsch, 93). Peer mediation has shown a decrease in classroom violence and verbal assault along with an increase in students' self-esteem (Harper, 93).	No study.
6. Conflict resolution programs.	There are school, community, and employer based programs. School-based conflict resolution programs have shown a decrease in classroom violence (Metis Associates, Inc., 88).	No study.
Services for Victims		
7. Advocacy.	There are programs for specific victim populations such as gay and lesbian action groups and the NAACP. However, there are no studies of the effectiveness of such programs (Herek and Berrill, 92; Wertheimer, 92).	No study.
Services for Offenders		
8. Criminal sanction and hate crimes reform.	The prosecution of offenders motivated by hate or bias is believed to help deter people from committing such crimes. There is no conclusive data available yet (Reiss and Roth, 93).	No study. ■

▌Methodology

We decided early in this process to review material that relates directly to the reduction of violence. There are many strategies for working with children and adults to increase their well-being or functioning; we did not try to make the connection to reduced violence unless the authors themselves suggested it. The literature review involved the following steps.

1. Identification of Literature

- Computer searches were done in the following reference databases: Psychological Abstracts, Sociological Abstracts, Medline, Criminal Justice Periodical Index, Educational Resources Information Center of the U.S. Department of Education (ERIC), and Public Affairs Information Services.

- We contacted the following organizations for bibliographies and references: National Center for Dispute Resolution, National Committee for Prevention of Child Abuse, National Rural Health Association, The Kempe Center for the Prevention and Treatment of Child Abuse, and The National Center on Child Abuse and Neglect.

- To locate materials that might not be found in the academic literature, we conducted additional searches through the Juvenile Justice Clearinghouse, the Rural Information Center Health Service Library, the Center for the Study and Prevention of Violence, and The National Crime Prevention Council.

2. Examination of the Literature

- Literature was sorted by topic areas: assault, rape, child abuse, and so forth.

- Literature was sorted into four categories: review literature, evaluation studies, descriptive material, or rural specific.

- Review literature was further studied for the reports they included, and when appropriate, these reports were sought. We included materials that focused on prevention, intervention, services for victims, services to reduce offender recidivism, and rural specific studies.

- Evaluation literature was then evaluated as to the strength of the research methodology and how closely the strategy came to actually reducing violence.

- Studies were categorized as showing: 1) substantial evidence of effectiveness in reducing violence or helping the victim; 2) moderate evidence of reducing violence or helping the victim; 3) moderate evidence of changing attitudes, knowledge and skills that may influence violence or victim trauma; and 4) strategies that are proposed by experts in the field but have not been tested.

3. Organization of Information

- Lists of intervention, prevention, and treatment programs that had been evaluated and shown to have some success were developed according to the seven violence categories.

- Some of the material related to more than one category. In such cases, we placed the information where it seemed most pertinent and cross-referenced it with other sections. ■

Adams, Regina Drake and Michael L. Benjamin

1988   "Innovative Approaches to Mental Health Service Delivery in Rural Areas." *Journal of Rural Community Psychology,* 9(2), 41-50.

Alexander, Pamela C., Robert A. Niemeyer, and Victoria M. Follette

1991   "Group Therapy for Women Sexually Abused as Children." *Journal of Interpersonal Violence,* 6(2), 218-231.

Ammerman, Robert and Michael Hersen

1990   *Treatment of Family Violence.* John Wiley and Sons, New York.

Andrews, D. A., Ivan Zinger, Robert D. Hoge, James Bonta, Paul Gendreau, and Francis T. Collin

1990   "Does Correctional Treatment Work? A Clinically Relevant and Psychologically Informed Meta-Analysis." *Criminology,* 28(3), 369-404.

Andrews, Janice

1990   "A Support Group for Rural Women Survivors of Domestic Violence." *Human Services in the Rural Environment,* 14(2), 39-42.

Bachman, Ronet

1992   *Crime Victimization in City, Suburban, and Rural Areas: A National Crime Victimization Survey Report,* U.S. Department of Justice, Office of Justice Programs, Washington, D.C.

Bachman, Ronet

1994   *Violence Against Women: A National Crime Victimization Survey Report,* U.S. Department of Justice, Office of Justice Programs, NCJ-145325, Washington, D.C.

Barth, Richard P.

1991   "An Experimental Evaluation of In-home Child Abuse Prevention Services." *Child Abuse and Neglect,* 15, 363-375.

Barth, Richard P., David S. Serezotes, and Holly E. Danforth

1991   "Preventing Adolescent Abuse." *Journal of Primary Prevention,* 11(3), 193-205.

Bartollas, Clemens

1985   *Correctional Treatment: Theory and Practice.* Prentice-Hall, Inc., Englwood Cliffs, New Jersey.

Bath, Howard I. and David Haapala

1993   "Intensive Family Preservation Services with Abused and Neglected Children: An Examination of Group Differences." *Child Abuse and Neglect*, 17, 213-225.

Becker, Judith and John A. Hunter, Jr.

1992   "Evaluation of Treatment Outcome for Adult Perpetrators of Child Sexual Abuse." *Criminal Justice and Behavior*, 19(1), 74-92.

Becker, Judith and Meg S. Kaplan

1992   "Research on Adolescent Sex Offenders." In Ann Wolbert Burgess (Ed.), *Child Trauma I: Issues and Research*, 383-404. Garland Publishing, Inc., New York.

Benoit, Jeffrey and Wallace Kennedy

1992   "The Abuse History of Male Adolescent Sex Offenders." *Journal of Interpersonal Violence*, 7(4), 543-548.

Bergman, Libby

1992   "Dating Violence among High School Students." *Social Work*, 37(1), 21-27.

Berkovitz, Irving H.

1985   "The Role of Schools in Child, Adolescent, and Youth Suicide Prevention." In M. L. Peck., N. L. Farberow, and R. E. Litman (Eds.), *Youth Suicide*, 170-190.

Berman, Alan L. and David A. Jobes

1991   *Adolescent Suicide: Assessment and Intervention*. American Psychological Association, Washington D.C.

Bleach, Gail and William L. Claiborn

1974   "Initial Evaluation of Hot-Line Telephone Crisis Centers." *Community Mental Health Journal*, 10(4), 387-394.

Bogal-Allbritten, Rosemarie and Lillian Rogers Daughaday

1990   "Spouse Abuse Program Services: A Rural-Urban Comparison." *Human Services in the Rural Environment*, 14(2), 6-10.

Brannon, James M. and Richard Troyer

1991   "Peer Group Counseling: A Normalized Residential Alternative to the Specialized Treatment of Adolescent Sex Offenders." *International Journal of Offender Therapy and Comparative Criminology*, 35(3), 225-234.

Bremer, Janis F.

1992   "Serious Juvenile Sex Offenders: Treatment and Long-term Follow-up." *Psychiatric Annals*, 22(6), 326-332.

Buzawa, Eva S. and Carl G. Buzawa

1990   *Domestic Violence: The Criminal Justice Response*. Sage Publications, Newbury Park, California.

Byrne, John K.
1977   "Social Integration, Conflict and Violence in Rural and Urban Families." Master thesis, University of New Hampshire, Department of Sociology.

California Criminal Justice Planning Office
1991   "Pilot Juvenile Sex Offender Treatment Program." Final Evaluation Report, May.

Caringella-MacDonald, Susan
1984   "Sexual Assault Prosecution: An Examination of Model Rape Legislation in Michigan." *Criminal Justice, Politics and Women*, 4(3), 65-82.

Carr, Kathleen et al.
1986   "An Elder Abuse Assessment Team in an Acute Hospital Setting." *Gerontologist*, 26, 115-118.

Center for Disease Control and Prevention
1992   *Youth Suicide Prevention Programs: A Resource Guide.* National Center for Injury Prevention and Control, Epidemiology Branch: Atlanta, Georgia, September.

Center for the Study of Youth Policy
1989   "Programs for Serious and Violent Juvenile Offenders." Institute for Social Research and Center for Study of Youth Policy, University of Michigan, Ann Arbor, Michigan.

Ciffone, Jeffrey
1993   "Suicide Prevention: A Classroom Presentation to Adolescents." *Social Work*, 38(2), 197-203.

Clark, Jacob R.
1993   "Where to Now on Domestic Violence? Studies Offer Mixed Policy Guidance." *Law Enforcement News,* April 30, XIX(379), 1, 17.

Connelly, Cynthia D. and Murray A. Straus
1992   "Mother's Age and Risk for Physical Abuse." *Child Abuse and Neglect*, 16, 709-718.

Connors, Gerard J.
1983   "Effect of Paraprofessional Contacts in Rural Parent Group Recruitment." *Journal of Rural Community Psychology*, 4(1), 35-42.

Curtis, Lynn A.
1987   a. "Preface." b. "The Retreat of Folly: Some Modest Replications of Inner-City Success." *The Annals of the American Academy of Political and Social Science*, 494, 71-89.

Daro, Deborah
1988   *Confronting Child Abuse: Research for Effective Program Design.* The Free Press, New York.

Davis, John M. and Jonathan Sandoval

1991   *Suicidal Youth.* Jossey-Bass Publishers, San Francisco.

Davis, Liane V. and Jan Hagen

1992   "The Problem of Wife Abuse: The Interrelationship of Social
Policy and Social Work Practice." *Social Work*, 3(1), 15-20.

Davis, Robert C. and Madeline Henley

1990   "Victim Service Programs." In A. J. Lurigio, W. G. Skogan
and R. C. Davis (Eds.), *Victims of Crime*, 157-171, Sage Publications, Newbury Park, California.

Derezotes, D. and Richard P. Barth

1993   "Adolescent Maltreatment Prevention." *Social Work in
Education*, 15(3), 151-166.

Deutsch, Morton

1993   "Educating for a Peaceful World." *American Psychologist*, 48(5),
510-517.

Dickstein, Leah and Nadelson, Carol (Eds.)

1989   *Family Violence: Emerging Issues of a National Crisis.*
American Psychiatric Press, Inc., Washington, D.C.

Diekstra, René

1992   "The Prevention of Suicidal Behavior: Evidence for the Efficacy
of Clinical and Community-Based Programs." *International
Journal of Mental Health*, 21(3), 69-87.

Dimock, Edmond

1980   "Youth Crisis Services: Short-Term Community-Based Residential Treatment." *Juvenile Justice in Rural America,* J. Jankoric
(Ed.), 111-117.

**Duluth Women's Coalition and Program for Aid to Victims of Sexual
Assault**

1991   "Teen Violence Prevention Projects." *High School Curriculum,*
November.

Dunford, Franklin W., David Huizinga and Delbert S. Elliott

1990   "The Role of Arrest in Domestic Assault: The Omaha Police
Experiment." *Criminology*, 28, 183-206.

Edleson, Jeffrey

1993   "Advocacy Services for Battered Women." *Violence Update*, 4(4),
1-10.

Edleson, Jeffrey L. and Richard M. Tolman

1992   *Intervention for Men Who Batter: An Ecological Approach.*
Sage Publications, Newbury Park, California.

Edleson, Jeffrey L.

1990   "Judging the Success of Interventions with Men Who Batter."
In D. J. Besharov (Ed.) *Family Violence: Research and Public
Policy Issues,* 130-145.

Edleson, Jeffrey L. and Marilyn Frank

1991 "Rural Interventions in Woman Battering: One State's Strategies." *Families in Society*, Nov., 543-551.

Eron, Leonard D.

1986 "Interventions to Mitigate the Psychological Effects of Media Violence on Aggressive Behavior." *Journal of Social Issues*, 42(3), 155-169.

Fagan, Jeffrey

1987 "Neighborhood Education, Mobilization, and Organization for Juvenile Crime Prevention." *The Annals of the American Academy of Political and Social Science*, 494, 54-70.

Fantuzzo, John W. and Anne Holland

1992 "Resilient Peer Training: Systematic Investigation of a Treatment." In *Child Trauma I, Issues and Research.* Ann Wolbert Burgess (Ed.), 739, 275-292. Garland Publishing, Inc., New York.

Farrington, David P., Lloyd E. Ohlin, and James Q. Wilson

1986 *Understanding and Controlling Crime: Toward a New Research Strategy.* Springer-Verlag, New York.

Finkelhor, David

1991 "Child Sexual Abuse." In M. Rosenberg and Fenley (Eds.), *Violence in America*, Oxford University Press, New York.

Fitzgerald, Edward A.

1990 "Chemical Castration: MPA Treatment of the Sexual Offender." *American Journal of Criminal Law*, 18(1), 1-60.

Foa, Edna, Barbara Olasov Rothbaum, and Gail Stekette

1993 "Treatment of Rape Victims." *Journal of Interpersonal Violence*, 8(2), 256-276.

Friedman, Lucy W. and Minna Shulman

1990 "Domestic Violence: The Criminal Justice Response." In A. J. Lurigio, W. G. Skogan and R. C. Davis (Eds.), *Victims of Crime*, 87-103. Sage Publications, Newbury Park, California.

Ganong, Lawrence H. and Marilyn Coleman

1983 "An Evaluation of the Use of Volunteers as Parent Educators." *Family Relations*, 32, 117-122.

Garbarino, James and Nancy Jacobson

1978 "Youth Helping Youth in Cases of Maltreatment of Adolescents." *Child Welfare*, 42(8), 505-510.

Garrison, C. Z., R. E. McKeown, R. F. Valors, and M. L. Vincent

1993 "Aggression, Substance Abuse, and Suicidal Behaviors in High School Students." *American Journal of Public Health*, 83(2), 179-183.

Gaudin, James, Jr.

1993   "Effective Intervention with Neglectful Families." *Criminal Justice and Behavior*, 20(1), 66-89.

Gaudin, James, Jr. and David Kurtz

1985   "Parenting Skills Training for Child Abusers." *Journal of Group Psychotherapy*, Psychodrama and Sociometry, 38(1), 35-54.

Gay and Lesbian Community Action Council

1992   "Crime victim advocates report of calls from greater Minnesota." Unpublished report, Minneapolis, Minnesota.

Geffner, Robert and Mildred Pagelow

1990   "Victims of Spouse Abuse." In Ammerman and Hersen (Eds.), *Treatment of Family Violence*, 113-135. John Wiley and Sons, New York.

Gerdean, Tan, Margaret Ray, and Rodney Cate

1991   "Migrant Farm Child Abuse and Neglect within an Ecosystem Framework." *Family Relations*, 40, 84-90.

Giacobbe, George A.

1988   "Length of Stay and Age Affect Recidivism after a Quality Treatment Program." *International Journal of Adolescence and Youth*, 1, 257-267.

Gingerich, Wallace J., Raymond J. Gurney, and Thomas S. Wirtz

1988   "How Helpful Are Helplines? A Survey of Callers." *Social Casework*, 69(10), 634-639.

Gold, Deborah T. and Lisa P. Gwyther

1989   "The Prevention of Elder Abuse: An Educational Model." *Family Relations*, 38, 8-14.

Goleman, Daniel

1991   "New Way to Battle Bias: Fight Acts, Not Feelings," *New York Times*, July 16.

Gondolf, Edward W.

1992   "Standards for Court Mandated Batterer Counseling: A Reply to Goldman." *Domestic Violence and Sexual Assault Bulletin*, 8(1), 18-21.

Grau, Janis, Jeffrey Fagan, and Sandra Wexter

1984   "Restraining Orders for Battered Women: Issues of Access and Efficacy." *Criminal Justice, Politics and Women*, 14(3), 13-28.

Graves, Roger, D. Kim Openshaw, and Gerald R. Adams

1992   "Adolescent Sex Offenders and Social Skills Training." *International Journal of Offender Therapy and Comparative Criminology*, 36(2), 139-152.

Grayson, Joann and Charlotte V. McNulty

1982   "Innovative Programming for Child Abuse and Neglect." *Journal of Rural Community Psychology*, 3(2), 35-41.

Greenwood, Peter W.

1982   "The Violent Offender in the Criminal Justice System."
In M. E. Wolfgang and N. A. Weiner (Eds.), *Criminal Violence*,
392-346. Sage Publications, Newbury Park, California.

Hagen, Michael and Robert P. King

1992   "Recidivism Rates of Youth Completing an Intensive Treatment
Program in a Juvenile Correctional Facility." *International
Journal of Offender Therapy and Comparative Criminology*,
36(4), 349-358.

Hamlin, Elwood R., II

1991   "Community-Based Spouse Abuse Protection and Family
Preservation Team." *Social Work*, 36(5), 402-406.

Hamm, Mark S.

1993   *American Skinheads: The Criminology and Control of Hate
Crime.* Praeger: West Port, Connecticut.

Hardy, J. B. and R. Strueett

1989   "Family Support and Parenting Education in the Home: An
Effective Extension of Clinic-Based Prevention Health Care
Services for Poor Children." *Journal of Pediatrics*, 115(6), 927-931.

Harper, Brian

1993   "Peer Mediation Programs: Teaching Students Alternatives to
Violence." *Journal of Dispute Resolution*, 2, 323-331.

Harvey, Mary R.

1985   *Exemplary Rape Crisis Programs: A Cross-Site Analysis and
Case Studies.* National Institute of Mental Health, Rockville,
Maryland.

Hawkins, J. David, Richard F. Catalano, Jr., and Associates

1992   *Communities That Care: Action for Drug Abuse Prevention.*
Jossey-Bass Publishers, San Francisco.

Hawkins, J. David, Elizabeth Von Cleve, and Richard F. Catalano

1991   "Reducing Early Childhood Aggression: Results of a Primary
Prevention Program." *Journal of the American Academy of
Child and Adolescent Psychiatry*, 30(2), 208-217.

Herek, Gregory and Kevin Berrill

1992   *Hate Crimes: Confronting Violence against Lesbians and Gay
Men.* Sage Publications, Newbury Park, California.

Hiebert-Murphy, Diane, Rayleen De Luca, and Marsha Runtz

1992   "Group Treatment for Sexually Abused Girls: Evaluating
Outcomes." *Families in Society: The Journal of Contemporary
Human Services*, April, 205-213.

Higgins, Paul S.

1994   "Victimization and School Safety for the St. Croix River
Education District." Report, Research Arts, Minneapolis.

Hilton, Zoe

1994   "The Failure of Arrest to Deter Wife Assault. What Now?" *Violence Update*, 4(5), 1-10.

Holub, M., S. Bauer, and W. Friedrich

1992   "Correlates of Adolescent Suicide Attempts." Working paper, Mayo Clinic, Rochester, Minnesota.

Howing, Phyllis T., John S. Woodarski, James M. Gaudin, Jr., and P. David Kurtz

1989   "Effective Interventions to Ameliorate the Incidence of Child Maltreatment: The Empirical Base." *Social Work*, 330-335.

Howitt, Pamela S. and Eugene Arthur Moore

1993   "Pay Now So You Won't Pay Later: The Effectiveness of Prevention Programming in the Fight to Reduce Delinquency." *Juvenile and Family Court Journal*, 44(2), 57-67.

Hughes, Honore M.

1986   "Child Focused Interventions in Shelters." Paper Presented at the Annual Convention of the American Psychological Association. August, Washington, D.C.

Izzo, Rhena K. and Robert R. Ross

1990   "Meta-Analysis of Rehabilitation Programs for Juvenile Delinquents." *Criminal Justice and Behavior*, 17(1), 134-142.

Jaffe, Peter, Marlies Sudermann, Deborah Reitzel, and Steve Killip

1992   "An Evaluation of a Secondary School Primary Prevention Program on Violence and Intimate Relationships." *Violence and Victims*, 7(2), 129-146.

Kenkel, Mary Beth

1986   "Stress-Coping-Support in Rural Communities: A Model for Primary Prevention." *American Journal of Community Psychology*, 14(5), 457-478.

Kimmel, Michael

1993   "Does Pornography Cause Rape?" *Violence Update*, 3(10), 1-10.

Kleck, Gary and E. Britt Patterson

1993   "The Impact of Gun Control and Gun Ownership Levels on Violence Rates." *Journal of Quantitative Criminology*, 9(3), 249-287.

Kline, Betty, Joann Grayson, and Virginia A. Mathie

1990   "Parenting Support Groups for Parents at Risk of Abuse and Neglect." *Journal of Primary Prevention*, 10(4), 313-319.

Kloss, James D.

1978   "The Impact of Comprehensive Community Treatment: An Assessment of the Complex Offender Project." *Offender Rehabilitation*, 3(1), 81-108.

Koss, Mary and Mary Harvey

1987 *The Rape Victim: Clinical and Community Approaches to Treatment*. Stephen Greene Press, Lexington, Massachusetts.

Kowal, Loretta W. Carol P. Kottmeier, Catherine C. Ayoub, Judith A. Komives, David S. Robinson, and Joseph P. Allen

1989 "Characteristics of Families at Risk of Problems: Findings from Home-Based Secondary Prevention Programs." *Child Welfare*, LXVIII(5), 529-538.

Kumpfer, Karole L.

1993 "Strengthening America's Families: Promising Parenting Strategies for Delinquency Prevention: User's Guide." Office of Juvenile Justice and Delinquency Prevention, Office of Juvenile Programs, U.S. Department of Justice, NCJ140781.

Lake, Elise S.

1993 "An Exploration of the Violent Victim Experiences of Female Offenders." *Violence and Victims*, 8(1), 41-51.

Larson, James D.

1992 "Anger and Aggression Management Techniques through the Think First Curriculum." *Journal of Offender Rehabilitation*, 18 (1/2), 101-117.

Levitt, Carolyn, Sally Couser, and Greg Owen

1994 *A Follow-up Study of Children Examined in 1985-1986 for Sexual Abuse: How Children Fare Eight Years Later*. Midwest Children's Resource Center, Children's Hospital, St. Paul, Minnesota, June.

Long, Kathleen A.

1986 "Suicide Intervention and Prevention within Indian Adolescent Populations." *Issues in Mental Health Nursing*, 8, 247-253.

Lucas, Emma T.

1991 *Elder Abuse and Its Recognition among Health Service Professionals*. Garland Publishing, Inc., New York.

Mackenzie, Doris Layton

1990 "BootCamp Prisons: Components, Evaluations and Empirical Issues." *Federal Probation*, 54(3), 44-52.

Mackenzie, Doris Layton, James W. Shaw, and Voncile B. Gowdy

1993 "An Evaluation of Shock Incarceration in Louisiana." National Institute of Justice: *Research in Brief*, June, 1-7.

Maguire, Mike

1991 "The Needs and Rights of Victims of Crime." *Crime and Justice: A Review of Research*, 14, 363-433.

McKernan McKay, Mary

1994 "The Link Between Domestic Violence and Child Abuse: Assessment and Treatment Considerations." *Child Welfare*, 73(1), 29-39.

Metis Associates, Inc.

1988   "The Resolving Conflicts Creatively Program: A Summary of Significant Findings." Unpublished report, New York, November.

Mills, Crystal S. and Barbara J. Granoff

1992   "Date and Acquaintance Rape among a Sample of College Students." *Social Work*, 37(6), 504-509.

Minnesota Department of Planning

1995   *Within Our Means: Tough Choices for Government Spending.* St. Paul, Minnesota.

Mooney, Kevin C.

1986   "Implementation and Evaluation of a Helping Skills Intervention in Five Rural Schools." *Journal of Rural Community Psychology*, 7(2), 27-36.

Morgan John R., Jeanette Nu-Man-Sheppard, and Diana Allin

1990   "Prevention through Parent Training: Three Parent Education Programs." *Journal of Primary Prevention*, 10(4), 321-331.

Motto, Jerry A.

1985   "Treatment Concerns in Preventing Youth Suicide." In M. L. Peck, N. L. Farberow, and R. E. Litman (Eds.), *Youth Suicide*, 91-111.

Mueller, Daniel and Paul S. Higgins

1988   *Funders Guide Manual: A Guide to Prevention Programs in Human Services, Focus on Children and Adolescents.* The Amherst H. Wilder Foundation, St. Paul, Minnesota.

Myers, John E. B.

1993   "Investigative Interviews of Children: Should They Be Videotaped?" *Notre Dame Journal of Law, Ethics, and Public Policy*, 7, 371-387.

Myers, Toby

1993   "Reoffending in Battering Intervention Programs." *Violence Update*, 4(3), 3, 8.

National Research Council

1993   *Understanding Child Abuse and Neglect*, Panel on Research on Child Abuse and Neglect, Commission on Behavioral and Social Sciences and Education, National Research Council.

Newberger, Eli

1991   "Child Abuse." In M. Rosenberg and Fenley (Eds.), *Violence in America*, Oxford University Press, New York.

Nightingale, Heath and Patrick Morrissette

1993   "Dating Violence: Attitudes, Myths, and Preventive Programs." *Social Work in Education*, 15(4), 225-232.

O'Carroll, Patrick, Mark L. Rosenberg, and James A. Mercy

1991 "Suicide." In M. Rosenberg and Fenley (Eds.), *Violence in America*, Oxford University Press, New York.

Office of Juvenile Justice and Delinquency Prevention

1993 "Comprehensive Strategy for Serious, Violent, and Chronic Juvenile Offenders." U.S. Department of Justice, Office of Justice Programs, Washington, D.C.

Olweus, Dan

1991 "Bully/Victim Problems among School Children: Basic Facts and Effects of a School-Based Intervention Program." In D. Pepler and K. Rubin (Eds.), *The Development and Treatment of Childhood Aggression*, Lawrence Erlbaum Associates, Hillsdale, New Jersey.

Owen, Greg and Paul Mattessich

1988 "Community Assistance Program: Results of a Controlled Study of the Effects of Non-Residential Correction Services on Adult Offenders in Ramsey County." Published report, Amherst H. Wilder Foundation, St. Paul, Minnesota.

Owens, Timothy

1984 "Bremer House Revisited: A Report on an Alternative Treatment Program of Young Adult Offenders." Published report, Amherst H. Wilder Foundation, St. Paul, Minnesota.

Patten, Sylvia B., Yvonne K. Gatz, Belin Jones, and Deborah L. Thomas

1989 "Posttraumatic Stress Disorder and the Treatment of Sexual Abuse." *Social Work*, May, 197-203.

Pillemer, Karl and Susan Frankel

1991 "Domestic Violence against the Elderly." In M. Rosenberg and Fenley (Eds.), *Violence in America*, Oxford University Press, New York.

Platt, Constance M.

1992 "Colorado's Standards for the Treatment of Domestic Violence Perpetrators." *Family Violence and Sexual Assault Bulletin*, 8(1), 17-18.

Prentky, Robert and Ann Wolbert Burgess

1992 "Rehabilitation of Child Molesters: A Cost Benefit Analysis." In Ann Wolbert Burgess (Ed.), *Child Trauma I: Issues and Research*, 417-442. Garland Publishing, Inc., New York.

Quinsey, Vernon L., Grant J. Harris, Marnie E. Rice, and Martin L. Lalumiére

1993 "Assessing Treatment Efficacy in Outcome Studies of Sex Offenders." *Journal of Interpersonal Violence*, 8(4), 512-523.

Ragland, John D. and Alan L. Berman

1990- "Farm Crisis and Suicide: Dying on the Vine?" *Omega,*
1991 22(3), 173-185.

Ray, Joann and Susan A. Murty

1990 "Rural Child Sexual Abuse Prevention and Treatment." *Human Services in a Rural Environment*, 13(4), 24-29.

Reiss, Albert J. and Jeffrey A. Roth (Eds.)

1993 *Understanding and Preventing Violence*, National Academy Press, Washington, D.C.

Rieth, Sarah M.

1990 "A New Model for the Treatment of Adult Survivors of Sexual Abuse." *The Victimology Handbook, Research Findings, Treatment, and Public Policy,* Emilio Viano (Ed.), 261-274. Garland Publishing, Inc., New York.

Roberts, Albert R.

1990 *Helping Crime Victims: Research, Policy, and Practice.* Sage Publications, Newbury Park, California.

Roberts, Albert R. and Michael J. Camasso

1991 "The Effect of Juvenile Offender Treatment Programs On Recidivism: A Meta-Analysis of 46 Studies." *Notre Dame Journal of Law, Ethics, and Public Policy*, 5, 421-441.

Rosen, Anita

1981 "Wife Abuse in Rural Areas: Some Social, Legal, Medical, and Service Delivery Issues." Paper Presented at the National Institute on Social Work in Rural Areas. July 26-29, Beaufort County, South Carolina.

Rosenbaum, Alan and Roland D. Maiuro

1990 "Perpetrators of Spouse Abuse." In Ammerman and Hersen (Eds.), *Treatment of Family Violence*, 280-309. John Wiley and Sons, New York.

Rosenberg, Mark L. and Mary Ann Fenley (Eds.)

1991 *Violence in America*, Oxford University Press, New York.

Rosenberg, Mark L. and James A. Mercy

1991 "Assaultive Violence." In M. Rosenberg and Fenley (Eds.), *Violence in America*, Oxford University Press, New York.

Rosenbluth, B.

1992 "Teen Dating Violence Project: 1991-1992, Final Report." The Center for Battered Women (Abstract), Austin, Texas, July.

Roth, Jeffrey A.

1994 "Pyschoactive Substances and Violence." *Research in Brief*, National Institute of Justice, February.

Roundtree, George A., Charles E. Grenier, and Virginia L. Hoffman

1993 "Parental Assessment of Behavioral Change after Children's Participation in a Delinquency Prevention Program." *Journal of Offender Rehabilitation*, 19, 113-130.

Rowsey, Jeanette, Orman Hall, and Eileen Coan

1984   "Rural Knowledge and Attitudes about Sexual Assault: The Impact of a Rape Awareness Campaign." *Journal of Rural Community Psychology*, 5(2), 33-54.

Sadoff, Robert L.

1986   "Sexual Violence." *Bulletin of the New York Academy of Medicine* 62(5), 466-476.

Sauter, Matthew J.

1993   "Post-Conviction Mediation of Rape Cases: Working within the Criminal Justice System to Achieve Well-Rounded Justice." *Journal of Dispute Resolution*, 1, 175-192.

Schechter, Lowell F.

1981   "The Benefits of Smallness: Developing a Model for an Effective Rural Child Protection Team." *Child Welfare*, LX, No. 3, 131-147.

Schlesinger, Benjamin and Rachel Schlesinger

1988   *Abuse of the Elderly, Issues and Annotated Bibliography.* University of Toronto Press, Toronto, Canada.

Schmidt, Janell and Lawrence Sherman

1993   "Does Arrest Deter Domestic Violence?" *American Behavioral Scientist,* 36(5), 601-609.

Schneider, Anne L.

1986   "Restitution and Recidivism Rates of Juvenile Offenders: Results from Four Experimental Studies." *Criminology*, 24(3), 533-552.

Schwartz, Barbara K.

1992   "Effective Treatment Techniques for Sex Offenders." *Psychiatric Annals*, 22(6), 315-319.

Sefcik, Thomas and Nancy J. Ormsby

1978   "Establishing a Rural Child Abuse/Neglect Treatment Program." *Child Welfare*, LVII(3), 187-195.

Shaffer, D.

1993   "Suicide: Risk Factors and the Public Health." *American Journal of Public Health*, 83(2), 171-172.

Shepard, Melanie

1992   "Predicting Batterer Recidivism Five Years after Community Intervention." *Journal of Family Violence*, 7(3), 167-178.

Shonholtz, Raymond

1987   "The Citizens' Role in Justice: Building a Primary Justice and Prevention System at the Neighborhood Level." *The Annals of the American Academy of Political and Social Science*, 494, 42-53.

Shybut, John

1982   "Use of Paraprofessionals in Enhancing Mental Health Service Delivery in Rural Settings." *Journal of Rural Community Psychology*, 3(1), 59-64.

Silver, Thelma and Howard Goldstein

1992   "A Collaborative Model of a County Crisis Intervention Team: The Lake County Experience." *Community Mental Health Journal*, 28(3), 249-256.

Sjolin, M. E. and Dave Riley

1993   *Parenting: The First Year Newsletter Series:* "Do Parents in Clark County Find the Project Helpful," Working Paper, University of Wisconsin Extension, Clark County.

Smets, Anton C.

1987   "A Group Treatment Program for Adolescent Sex Offenders: Five Steps toward Resolution" *Child Abuse and Neglect,* 11, 247-254.

Sorenson, Susan B. and Jacequelyn White

1992   "Adult Sexual Assault: Overview of Research." *Journal of Social Issues*, 48(1), 1-8.

Stark, Evan and Anne H. Flitcraft

1991   "Spouse Abuse." In M. Rosenberg and Fenley (Eds.), *Violence in America*, Oxford University Press, New York.

Stith, Sandra M., Mary Beth Williams, and Karen H. Rosen (Eds.)

1990   *Violence Hits Home: Comprehensive Treatment Approaches to Domestic Violence,* Springer Publishing Company, New York.

Stout, Karen D.

1991   "Intimate Femicide: A National Demographic Overview." *Journal of Interpersonal Violence,* 6(4), 476-485.

Straus, Murray A. and Richard Gelles (Eds.)

1990   *Physical Violence in American Families: Risk Factors and Adaptations to Violence in 8,145 Families,* Transaction Publishers, New Brunswick, New Jersey.

Syers, Maryann and Jeffrey L. Edleson

1992   "The Combined Effects of Coordinated Criminal Justice Intervention in Women Abuse." *Journal of Interpersonal Violence,* 7(4), 490-502.

Tutty, Leslie, Bruce Bidgood, and Michael Rothery

1993   "Support Groups for Battered Women: Research on Their Efficacy." *Journal of Family Violence*, 8(4), 325-342.

Umbreit, Mark S.

1993   "Balanced Approaches/Restorative Justice Project." Working Paper. University of Minnesota, Minneapolis, Minnesota.

Umbreit, Mark S.

1989 "Violent Offenders and Their Victims." *Mediation and Criminal Justice Victims, Offenders and Community.* Martin Wright and Bart Galaway (Eds.), Sage Publications, Newbury Park, California.

Umbreit, Mark S. and Robert B. Coates

1992 "Victim Offender Mediation: An Analysis of Programs in Four States of the U.S." Report, Citizens Council on Crime and Justice, Minneapolis, Minnesota.

U.S. Department of Justice

1992 "Crime Victimization in City, Suburban, and Rural Areas," Bureau of Justice Statistics, Washington, D.C.

U.S. Department of Justice

1965 *Sourcebook of Criminal Justice Statistics,* Bureau of Justice Statistics, Washington, D.C.

U.S. Department of Justice

1970 *Sourcebook of Criminal Justice Statistics,* Bureau of Justice Statistics, Washington, D.C.

U.S. Department of Justice

1975 *Sourcebook of Criminal Justice Statistics,* Bureau of Justice Statistics, Washington, D.C.

U.S. Department of Justice

1980 *Sourcebook of Criminal Justice Statistics,* Bureau of Justice Statistics, Washington, D.C.

U.S. Department of Justice

1985 *Sourcebook of Criminal Justice Statistics,* Bureau of Justice Statistics, Washington, D.C.

U.S. Department of Justice

1990 *Sourcebook of Criminal Justice Statistics,* Bureau of Justice Statistics, Washington, D.C.

U.S. Department of Justice

1992 *Sourcebook of Criminal Justice Statistics,* Bureau of Justice Statistics, Washington, D.C.

Vass, Anthony A.

1990 *Alternatives to Prison: Punishment Custody and the Community.* Sage Publications, Newbury Park, California.

Von, Judith M., Dean G. Kilpatrick, Ann W. Burgess, and Carol R. Hartman

1991 "Rape and Sexual Assault." In M. Rosenberg and Fenley (Eds.), *Violence in America*, Oxford University Press, New York.

Walker, Lenore E. A.

1992   "Battered Women Syndrome and Self-Defense." *Notre Dame Journal of Law, Ethics, and Public Policy*, 6, 321-334.

Warner, Jody E. and David J. Hansen

1994   "The Identification and Reporting of Physical Abuse by Physicians: A Review and Implications for Research." *Child Abuse and Neglect*, 18, 11-25.

Weingrourt, Rita

1985   "Wife Rape: Barriers to Identification and Treatment." *American Journal of Psychotherapy*, 39(2), 187-192.

Wertheimer, David

1992   "Treatment and Service Interventions for Lesbian and Gay Male Crime Victims." In Gregory Herek and Berrill (Eds.). *Hate Crimes: Confronting Violence against Lesbians and Gay Men*, Sage Publications, Newbury Park, California.

Wesch, David and John Lutzker

1991   "A Comprehensive 5-Year Evaluation of Project 12 Ways: An Ecobehavioral Program for Treating and Preventing Child Abuse and Neglect." *Journal of Family Violence*, 6(1), 17-35.

Wheeler, Sandra, Nancee Neel, Doris Barnett, and Martha Jinright

1992   "Gift of Life: Enhancing the Availability of Obstetrical Care in Alabama." *Journal of Health Care for the Poor and Underserved*, 3, 7-20.

Whitcomb, Debra

1992   "When the Victim Is a Child," 2nd Ed. U.S. Department of Justice Programs, National Institute of Justice, Washington, D.C.

Williams-White, Deborah

1989   "Self-help and Advocacy: An Alternative Approach to Helping Battered Women." In L. Dickstein and C. Nadelson (Eds.), *Family Violence: Emerging Issues of a National Crisis*, 47-59. American Psychiatric Press, Inc., Washington, D.C.

Wilson, Margo and Martin Daly

1993   "Spousal Homicide Risk and Estrangement." *Violence and Victims*, 8(1), 3-16.

Wolf, Rosalie S. and Karl A. Pillemer

1989   *Helping Elderly Victims: The Reality of Elder Abuse.* Columbia University Press, New York. ■

INDEX

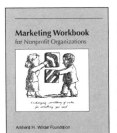